Terry - V

blessed so you may be a

blessing each day!

Your brother in-Christ,

MW01222210

Previously Published Works:

There Are No McDonald's In Heaven: Waiting on God
[WestBow Press; July 2012]

Thoughts From A Random Mind – Volume 1
[WestBow Press; January 2013]

MAN'S REJECTION OF GOD

WHO'S RESPONSIBLE?

RL Keller

WESTBOW®
PRESS
A DIVISION OF THOMAS NELSON
& ZONDERVAN

Copyright © 2014 RL Keller.

All rights reserved. No part of this book may be used or reproduced by any means,
graphic, electronic, or mechanical, including photocopying, recording, taping or by any
information storage retrieval system without the written permission of the publisher
except in the case of brief quotations embodied in critical articles and reviews.

All word definitions are taken from either
www.merriam-webster.com and www.oxforddictionary.com.

All Scripture quotations, unless otherwise indicated, are taken from the *Holy Bible,*
New International Version®. *NIV*®. Copyright © 1973, 1978, 1984 by International
Bible Society. Used by permission of Zondervan. All rights reserved.

Scripture quotations marked "ESV" have been taken from *The Holy Bible, English*
Standard Version. Copyright © 2000; 2001 by Crossway Bibles, a division of
Good News Publishers. Used by permission. All rights reserved.

Scripture quotations marked "MSG" have been taken from *THE MESSAGE*. Copyright © by Eugene H.
Peterson 1993, 1994, 1995, 1996, 2000, 2001, 2002. Used by permission of NavPress Publishing Group.

Scripture quotations marked "NASB" have been taken from the *New American*
Standard Bible, © Copyright 1960, 1962, 1963, 1968, 1971, 1972, 1973,
1975, 1977 by The Lockman Foundation. Used by permission.

Scripture quotations marked "NKJV" have been taken from the New King James Version.
Copyright © 1982 by Thomas Nelson, Inc. Used by permission. All rights reserved.

WestBow Press books may be ordered through booksellers or by contacting:

WestBow Press
A Division of Thomas Nelson & Zondervan
1663 Liberty Drive
Bloomington, IN 47403
www.westbowpress.com
1 (866) 928-1240

Because of the dynamic nature of the Internet, any web addresses or links contained
in this book may have changed since publication and may no longer be valid. The views
expressed in this work are solely those of the author and do not necessarily reflect the views
of the publisher, and the publisher hereby disclaims any responsibility for them.

Any people depicted in stock imagery provided by Thinkstock are models,
and such images are being used for illustrative purposes only.
Certain stock imagery © Thinkstock.

ISBN: 978-1-4908-2148-1 (sc)
ISBN: 978-1-4908-2149-8 (hc)
ISBN: 978-1-4908-2147-4 (e)

Library of Congress Control Number: 2014900343

Printed in the United States of America.

WestBow Press rev. date: 01/15/2014

Special Thanks

I would like to take this opportunity to thank those who have blessed me and made my life richer as a result of knowing them. First, I must thank God, for without the gifts He has bestowed upon me I could never have written even one book, let alone three. Next I need to thank Kissa, for she has been my anchor and great source of loving support. I love you & thank the Lord for you. You are a huge blessing to me. I also need to mention my dear friend, prayer partner and mentor, Royce Caskey, who has always had a listening ear. He has chastised me a time or two, and rightfully so, but has never judged me … not even once. I would be remiss not to mention my pastor and friend, Reverend Joseph Hein (or Pastor Joe as we call him). His friendship and acceptance has bolstered my faith and encouraged me in my efforts to do great things for God. Lastly, I would like to thank my publicist, friend and sister in Christ Helen Cook for her advice and wisdom. I couldn't have done anything of any value for God without all your support, prayers, advice and guidance. I thank God for you all.

Your loving friend and brother in Christ,
Rich

CONTENTS

Introduction ix

Chapter 1   Who Are We Really?... 1
Chapter 2   Atheists.. 10
Chapter 3   Agnostics...24
Chapter 4   Apostates..38
Chapter 5   Hedonists...46
Chapter 6   Homosexuality 56
Chapter 7   The Cult of Personality 66
Chapter 8   Buddhism, Hinduism & Islam 77
Chapter 9   What about sin? 91
Chapter 10   Relatability 100
Chapter 11   Consequences... 111
Chapter 12   Vulnerability 122
Chapter 13   Minimalism & Individualism 131
Chapter 14   Words 141
Chapter 15   The Needy Among Us...................................149
Chapter 16   Forgiveness 158
Chapter 17   Jesus & C.S. Lewis 166
Chapter 18   Are Christians the Problem? 176

INTRODUCTION

Our lives as Christians are in the spotlight quite a bit. The more famous the Christian, the more scrutiny they receive. We may not think we are being watched, but we would be wrong. People have their eye on us all the time. They point out our flaws and shrug off our good deeds. This book is an effort to look at what makes people turn away from God and whose fault it might be for their resistance to "religion". Many times the very people who are supposed to be trying to show folks the way to God are pushing them away by their words and actions. I haven't done any lengthy anthropological studies about the behavior of man, but I *have* lived my life among believers and non-believers for over fifty years and think I might just have some interesting insights into what we could be doing wrong and as a result why we are being ignored.

In *Man's Rejection of God: Who's Responsible?*, I devote whole chapters to Atheists, Agnostics, Apostates, Hedonists, those devoted to the Cult of Personality and more. I look at the three main world religions besides Judaism and Christianity. I give the reader a brief look into their belief system and how it compares to that of Christians. I touch on those who say they believe in God yet show no visible evidence of it. I investigate our being able to relate to others outside the faith. I lay out what it means to be vulnerable. I take a look at minimalism and individualism and how they can apply to the Christian. I look at the impact words have on our lives and also dig into the importance of forgiveness. I paint a simple picture of Jesus and underscore that picture with quotes from the great CS Lewis. In the end, we should be able to answer the question of just what the issues are. Once we have a little better understanding of those we are trying to reach, perhaps we can then give *ourselves* a makeover.

This is a serious topic with eternal ramifications, yet *not* one that we have to handle in a restrictive, regimented manner. It isn't our responsibility to save each person we encounter on a daily basis; God does the saving. It *is* however our responsibility to live a life that reveals God to others, all the while being prepared to give an account of the hope that is within us (1 Peter 3:15). God wants to use us, but we have to listen to Him. We are not in control, He is. God has to be because He is the only one who knows the condition of the heart of the person you are about to speak with. Allow me to speak to you through this book in a frank manner that could possibly revitalize your sagging testimony. You must have a teachable spirit to learn anything from God. You *can* be more like Christ. It's God's desire for us all.

I will say what I do each time I write a book; I am no different than you. I struggle with some of the some types of trials and tribulations as the rest of humanity. If you love the Lord, than we are brothers and sisters in Christ. I don't write this book to lord it over anyone, for like Paul, I am the chief of sinners. I wrestle with my old nature on a continual basis, just like you. I've been trying to be more like Christ each day. Let's do it together.

Your brother in Christ,
RL Keller

I would like to make one final statement: This God I serve continues to be an enigma of sorts. I'll never understand why He is so patient and gracious to me as long as I live. I suppose I am no better or worse than anyone else He has created, yet the mercy He extends to me is baffling. I don't deserve it; none of us do. Having said that I quickly confess that

I am and shall forever be eternally grateful for all the grace, mercy and loving kindness He has extended to me. Being one who does not play favorites, these gifts are yours as well. Let me close with this portion of scripture:

> "We know that the law is spiritual; but I am unspiritual, sold as a slave to sin. I do not understand what I do. For what I want to do I do not do, but what I hate I do. And if I do what I do not want to do, I agree that the law is good. As it is, it is no longer I myself who do it, but it is sin living in me. I know that good itself does not dwell in me, that is, in my sinful nature. For I have the desire to do what is good, but I cannot carry it out. For I do not do the good I want to do, but the evil I do not want to do—this I keep on doing. Now if I do what I do not want to do, it is no longer I who do it, but it is sin living in me that does it. So I find this law at work: Although I want to do good, evil is right there with me. For in my inner being I delight in God's law; but I see another law at work in me, waging war against the law of my mind and making me a prisoner of the law of sin at work within me. What a wretched man I am! Who will rescue me from this body of death? Thanks be to God, who delivers me through Jesus Christ our Lord! (Romans 7:14-25)

CHAPTER 1

WHO ARE WE REALLY?

A youth pastor went to visit a congregation member in the hospital. The woman he visited had a roommate who was a young woman in her mid to late 20's who had a pack of cigarettes on the stand next to her bed. After visiting with and praying for the congregation member the youth pastor turned to leave. He stopped by the foot of the bed of the roommate and said, "You know, smoking is bad for your health." After introducing himself, the youth pastor invited her to church and then promptly left.

> "I like your Christ. I do not like your Christians. Your Christians are so unlike your Christ." – **Mahatma Gandhi**

Is there a problem with the way Christians are portraying the gospel to the unsaved today? Are we driving people away from God? If not, why are non-believers turning a deaf ear to our message? If so, then what exactly is the problem? Why are Christians largely considered hypocrites to the unbelievers in society? We know God isn't the problem. Could it be that our delivery has something to do with it? It is my assertion that it does.

Throughout the New Testament we see no evidence that Jesus treated non-believers the way we treat them today. It's a mystery to me why we brow beat and judge people outside our faith, when we aren't treated that way by God. Jesus was compassionate, merciful, patient and kind as He instructed the masses that followed Him. Where do we get this whole "turn or burn" mentality? I have no earthly idea. We could debate the topic all day into the night and not come up with anything as straightforward as the example Christ gave us. It's interesting to note that His example didn't include browbeating unbelievers.

Back to the Basics

In baseball, many times when players are having a difficult time with some aspect of their game their coach has them go back to working on the basics. I think we need to do the same thing here; let's start with conversion and go from there.

When a person becomes a Christian, they are born again of the spirit. Jesus describes the process to a man named Nicodemus in John 3:1-21. We receive Christ into our hearts and lives by verbal consent. As a result, we experience the cleansing power of the Holy Spirit as all our sins are washed away. A genuine conversion by faith will result in an inner transformation. This dramatic change is both instantaneous and progressive. God sees us as holy and righteous immediately after our conversion; free from sin, based on the blood Christ shed. *That* part is instantaneous. Our actual transformation takes place like a moth turning into a beautiful butterfly. *That* part takes time and thus, is progressive. An immediate result of our inner change is that our demeanor begins to change; we begin to exude kindness rather than coarseness. We have a sense of tranquility within our spirit that wasn't there before. We begin to see that which is around us differently. As the progression begins we stumble and fall like any toddler just learning to walk. Over time, as we feed our spirit man, we slowly begin to learn to calm our spirit and rest. This is important so we can begin to know what God would have us do for Him. This can take months, even years. It's important for us to get into the habit of reading scripture. At times it won't come easily; it is an acquired habit, like regular exercise or eating properly. We need to ask God to expand our mind and speak to our spirit. We need to learn to do more listening than talking because we learn nothing new when we're talking. The whole idea is to emulate Christ in everything we think, say and do. We will never be perfect as He is perfect, but that's no reason not to strive for it. Once we are ready to present the gospel, we must do it with patience, kindness and mercy. If our listener blows us off they can never say they weren't told. They aren't rejecting us; they are rejecting the One who sent us.

We should never stop learning from the Lord; however, it requires an effort on our part. We won't receive wisdom and knowledge through osmosis. If we don't seek God's instruction and guidance we will stagnate, just like a pond does when no fresh water flows into it.

If we are going to make any difference in the name of the Lord, our underpinning must be Christ. We allow too many externals to influence us. We must educate ourselves regarding who we are *in* Christ. Once we know who we are, we need to find out what He wants us to accomplish in His name.

When I lived in Texas I saw something I had never seen before. It's called a 'turnabout' and it works like this: if you need to make a U-turn for any reason you go in a special lane that bypasses the lights. This lane takes you under the overpass, putting you on the service road facing the opposite direction. That's kind of what happens to the new believer; a 180-degree turnabout takes place in their life. This turnabout of a spiritual nature can cause families to divide, friendships to crumble and alliances to be destroyed.

I once dated a girl who was a Christian. Her parents attended church yet didn't have a personal relationship with Christ. As a result, the girl's mother told her one time that she would prefer she were "addicted to heroin then be a born-again Christian." Another time she said to her if she knew her daughter would have become "born-again" she would have aborted her. Because of the strife that her conversion caused within her family, she turned away from the Lord and ended up marrying an unsaved man.

That is a real life example of why we need to feed our spirit man daily so our roots drive down deep into the soil of the spirit. Pressure can be enormous when it comes to serving Christ. We must be well grounded spiritually and realize that we may lose much to follow Him. Without spiritual sustenance our underpinning will break loose, casting us adrift. At times we will need to make difficult decisions that may even involve walking away from our families to serve Christ. Not everyone will embrace your conversion with the same excitement and fervor that you do. Being well grounded will help you withstand the pressure that can come.

Free Will

Roughly thirty years ago I was still a new Christian. I wasn't an evangelistic dynamo, so witnessing didn't come very easy for me. I had been told we should witness to everyone we encountered in our day or we weren't being a good Christian. Not knowing any better I fumbled and stumbled my way through many a failed witness attempt, looking foolish and rarely making much sense. I submit to you that I wasn't ready. I didn't understand what I believed well enough. We must allow ourselves to grow and mature spiritually. There is no quick fix for this; our spiritual growth must be cultivated like a garden. We need to determine in our heart that we are going to serve the Lord no matter what. God will cause us to succeed in all we do if we strive to live for Him.

We are born with a free will to think and act as we choose. That carries over to spiritual things as well. There are a wide variety of belief systems that come under the title of "religion" today and we can believe whatever we choose to believe. Christians are one voice crying out among many voices with a message that we believe to be life changing. How we present that message can make all the difference in the world.

Jeremiah 29:11 tells us "For I know the plans I have for you," declares the LORD, "plans to prosper you and not to harm you, plans to give you hope and a future." Going out half-cocked with our feeble, untested faith can potentially bring disastrous results. While it's true that God's word accomplishes the purposes for which it is sent (Isaiah 55:11), we can present that word incorrectly or with blunt force and drive away those in need.

I knew a man who was involved in his church. He would do just about anything for the brethren, yet at his job he was rude, crass, insulting and extremely un-Christ-like to his co-workers. When I saw this side of him for the first time, I was taken aback. I didn't expect him to be perfect, but his words and actions didn't represent his Christian status in any way, shape or form. In fact, it was so contrary to his Sunday morning demeanor that you couldn't even tell he was a follower of Christ. I know of two other examples that are just like that. How many souls will never enter heaven because of their harsh words or actions?

While it pays for us to learn from another's bad example, we can only control our own words and actions. We need be attentive to the Holy Spirit to achieve self-control regarding this. The Bible tells us how to treat others, yet we insist on doing it our own way. I wish I knew why?

God knows how to minister to those who need to know Him; we do not. Everyone is different. We are all unique, made that way by God's own hand. We're different for a reason. For one, it makes life a lot more interesting. A world filled with people just like me is a very scary thought. This world wants to dictate the direction it takes all on its own, without interference from anyone, including this God Christians talk about. God wants to come first. That's where the rub lies. Even as Christians we strain at the leash not wanting God to make important, life-changing decisions that must be made in our lives. Knowing us intimately means God surely must know what's best for us, yet we struggle with the concept that He knows us better than we could ever know ourselves. Trying to convey that concept to individuals who have grown up outside the church can be very difficult. The non-believer will fight for their independence never realizing that they are enslaved to that which they are most involved. Other things in their lives have replaced God whether they know it or not. The root problem is that they simply don't want to be told what to do. This is an obstacle in reaching them with the gospel, but hammering away at them isn't the answer. Obstacles can be overcome and God knows how.

As believers we must pray for wisdom and discernment. We are going into the spiritual fray at a disadvantage. We are already thought of as hypocrites before we even open our mouths. All we can do is be genuine at all times to all people. Be honest, truthful, dependable, responsible and of high integrity. I didn't always represent Christ very well. My integrity was shaky; I did it to myself. God is forgiving; man tends not to be. We pay the consequences and move on trying to show others that even a person who falls off a horse can get back up and ride another day. Being humble is a key; showing the grace and mercy of God to all is important as well. These are characteristics that are acquired through experience. When we stumble and fall we represent the common man who fails, letting others know that nothing can void out God's love for them. People who see themselves as unworthy are hard to convince. The Holy Spirit must speak to their hearts and do the convincing.

Wrong approach

It's my contention that our approach is very much different than the approach used on us when we received Christ. The way we present the gospel message is inconsistent, as our lives become a blurry reflection of what it could be in Christ. Let me tell you something; the world is noticing. Those in the world are not like God in that they do **not** know our heart's motivation and **do** expect perfection from Christians. We judge without a moment's hesitation, never once considering the fact that God has never judged us either before or after our conversion. We need to accept that some folks will never believe in Christ or receive His forgiveness. It's a fact that some folks are simply contentious by nature. As they say in Texas, they would *"argue with a post, then pull up the post and argue with the hole"*. Our passion to serve God must be tempered by spiritual discernment and wisdom or we are destined to fail.

What about us would compel people to listen to what we have to say? Are we a positive example of Christ to the unbelieving world or nothing more than a clanging cymbal? If we're going to make a lasting impact in this world for Christ we need to figure that out. It starts with submission.

There are so many people out there that have problems and feel that God doesn't care because they see no evidence of His presence in their lives. The ones who can relate with these types of people are those who have been where they have been and come out of it. I can relate to people who have been divorced, because I have been divorced twice. I've never done drugs of any kind, but there are others who have and can relate to that type of problem. I did pull in a six-figure income at one point in my life and lost it all. I have also been deep in debt at one time. There are so many different areas of life that believers have come out of. A humble and submissive attitude to God's Spirit can make us a positive voice to those who feel they're the only ones stuck in the mud.

Christians seem prone to judging by sight rather than showing mercy in spite of what they see with their own eyes. We believe in an unseen deity without use of our eyes, why do we treat people like outsiders just because they might look or act different then us. We must learn to see *all* others the same way God does. This is also an acquired trait and one worthy of striving for.

Our church leaders prove they are human by saying one thing and doing another. I've known pastors who have purposely mislead or even out and out lied to their congregations. I have seen many not walk their talk, myself included. We condemn instead of show mercy. With self-righteous fury we shoot our own wounded by heaping condemnation on those brothers or sisters who have become entangled in some sort of sin. We pull the trigger rather than comfort them and show them support, leading them to repentance. If we would do that to fellow Christians, is it any surprise we lower the boom on non-believers? In Galatians 6:1 the Apostle Paul tells the church to *restore gently* those members who are caught up in sin. He also implores them to be careful so as not to become entangled themselves. I must confess that some of the 'Christians' I have known throughout my life would have actually kept me from receiving Christ had I not already become a believer.

In the end, whether a person believes or not is out of our control. We believe they need God. They are resistant. We should be more intent of *being* Jesus to others then spouting scripture to them. Our genuineness must be linked closely with consistency. We must actually be who we say we are and not pretend, because the world can see right through phonies. Do we really want to be just like everyone else?

———◦———

"In a portrait of the "unchurched" in America, a new study found that most are willing to hear what people have to say about Christianity but a majority also sees the church as a place full of hypocrites." [1]

CHAPTER 2

ATHEISTS

A man went to a barbershop to have his hair cut and his beard trimmed. As the barber began to work, they began to have a good conversation. They talked about so many things and various subjects. When they eventually touched on the subject of God, the barber said: 'I don't believe that God exists.' 'Why do you say that?' asked the customer. 'Well, you just have to go out in the street to realize that God doesn't exist. Tell me, if God exists, would there be so many sick people? Would there be abandoned children? If God existed, there would be neither suffering nor pain. I can't imagine a loving God who would allow all of these things.' The customer thought for a moment, but didn't respond because he didn't want to start an argument. The barber finished his job and the customer left the shop.

Just after he left the barbershop, he saw a man in the street with long, stringy, dirty hair and an untrimmed beard. He looked dirty and unkempt. The customer turned back and entered the barbershop again and he said to the barber: 'You know what? Barbers do not exist.' 'How can you say that?' asked the surprised Barber. 'I am here, and I am a barber. And I just worked on you!' 'No!' the customer exclaimed. 'Barbers don't exist because if they did, there would be no people with dirty long hair and untrimmed beards, like that man outside.' 'Ah, but barbers DO exist! That's what happens when people do not come to me.' 'Exactly!' affirmed the customer. 'That's the point! That's why there's so much pain and suffering in the world. God DOES exist! That's what happens when people don't go to Him and don't look to Him for help. '

What Is An Atheist?

If a 'theist' believes in the existence of a god(s), then putting an 'a' in front of the title would make it the antithesis; namely those who do *not* believe in the existence of a god(s). In spite of their disbelief, Christians believe God created atheists along with the rest of creation. Just because atheists refuse to accept that doesn't negate what we consider to be a reality. It's a faith issue. Atheists consistently bellow that they want believers in God to prove His existence. Because it's the cornerstone of a Christian's faith-based belief system, they shoot at the heart of it with the notion that they can cripple our faith with their relentless insistence. They can't prove He doesn't exist either, but that is supposed to be beside the point. Faith doesn't require proof for that would be a contradiction.

Recently, I asked the question "why don't people believe in God?" Not surprisingly, the bulk of the responses spoke of a need for proof; hard, cold facts, as with science. Facts don't require faith. Facts are uncovered by man and are subject to human error. Now non-believers point out that the men who wrote the Bible were human so scripture is subject to human error as well. While that is essentially a true statement, it's a little more complicated than that. When we believe in God, His word becomes alive to us. When we read a verse like "All Scripture is God-breathed and is useful for teaching, rebuking, correcting and training in righteousness" from 2 Timothy 3:16, we accept that scripture came to us through mortal man hand chosen by God. Therefore we accept that scripture is God-breathed or from the actual mouth of God. Again, this is a faith issue. If you don't believe in God you won't believe anything related to ones belief in God.

Hebrews 11, often referred to as "The Faith Chapter", gives us a clear-cut and concise definition of faith. Verse 1 tells us *"Now faith is confidence in what we hope for and assurance about what we do not see."* No proof need be sought for none shall be found; not in a faith-based belief system. Martin Luther King, Jr. put it this way: *"Faith is taking the first step even when you don't see the whole staircase."*

An atheist's god is science. They believe all truths can be found through a preponderance of theories they view as evidence proving the existence or nonexistence of this or that. God either exists or He doesn't. God gave us a free will meaning we get to choose what we believe. He wants willing followers, not ones who feel required to follow Him.

It should be no secret that atheists are actively attempting to erase God from man's conscientiousness by having Him removed from public life. I believe this all stems from an ever so slight twinge of conviction brought on by their refusal to accept the only one who can make it go away. Perhaps they feel the need to eradicate the very thought of God in the hopes that the twinge will stop. Otherwise, why would they care if people believed in God or not?

Evolution

Atheists espouse the validity of the evolution of man, rather than the Christian belief that the hand of God created all. Evolution is nothing more than a series of theories that are embraced by men who refuse to believe in any other explanation as to how we came into existence. Their belief in these theories doesn't make them true. Theories are not facts. If so, they would be called facts and not theories. These folks have placed their faith in their own hypothesis.

Christians place their faith in ancient writings that have been passed down and bound into one book called the Bible. It's really all a matter of what you choose to believe. Christians have chosen to place their faith in an unseen God. Through the scriptures we learn who God is and who we are *in* Him. We also learn that His Son, Jesus Christ, died for our sins so that we might live with Him forever. For that we are mocked. Society mocks those things they do not or in this case cannot comprehend. Not wanting to accept what they don't understand, they lash out at it, for it disrupts their order of things.

Proverbs 14:12 & 16:25 utter the same warning for all created beings: "There is a way that seems right to a man, but in the end it leads to death." Flawed men use flawed logic to come up with flawed plans that even if they should happen to succeed provide limited satisfaction for the world is ever changing. Time never stops. New dilemmas or challenges inevitably confront man, at times on a daily basis. The only way to avoid the challenges of life is to divorce yourself from society and disengage from life altogether. That would leave you as a solitary lump of human flesh sitting on your couch doing nothing. That is no way to live a life.

Standards

Atheists say that if God *did* exist He could and would stop all the evil, death, violence and destruction. Because it exists, there can be no God. They have a faulty understanding of who God is and how He operates. Christians don't believe God is the author of evil, although He *allows* it for His own purposes. If God doesn't exist, then what causes all the evil, death, violence and destruction that occurs in the world. The condition of this world shines a light on the fact that man apart from God is inherently evil. Man's inhumanity to man would be a direct result of the darkness of men's hearts, which is the result of sin or the disobedience of the standard that has been set by God. One point that atheists fail to consider is that in reality, some of the most heinous, despicable events in history were done by people who didn't believe in God; Joseph Stalin and Mao Tse Tung to name just two.

> *"This is the crisis we're in: God's light streamed into the world, but men and women everywhere ran for the darkness … because they were not really interested in pleasing God."*
> (John 3:19; MSG)

It's a fallacy to believe that men can coexist without a code of ethics and morals. Peace and harmony are simply unattainable without some sort of universal standard. 'Anything goes' eventually leads to wanton chaos, which may be enjoyed by some, but would hardly be acceptable to the majority. The existence of chaos begs the question 'what standard is being used?' It's difficult to survive without boundaries and rules. Standards provide structure and structure provides order, which leads to civility and rational thought. Chaos leads to anarchy and lawlessness. Those that desire chaos desire it solely to gain ultimate and absolute control over the masses.

If we can agree that standards are needed, who would set up those standards? It's an enigmatic situation. Atheists don't believe in God, yet still need some sort of rules to follow; a compass to help them determine what's right and wrong. Will we rely solely on the government to determine this for us? That smacks of Socialism. If not the government, then who? Who shall determine what great mind will sort out all of life's issues and give mankind a guide for living? If a person is chosen, how do we know he is the right choice? Someone needs to lead. If we say that man can govern himself, what standard would *he* use? You see, we keep coming back to the same problem over and over. Without standards, there's chaos. We all can't develop our own set of individual standards.

God sets a standard that we can all live by in the Ten Commandments. Although I have enough trouble meeting those standards, at least I know what I'm dealing with. I know that by reading the Bible. Atheists say we are wasting our time reading a fictitious book filled with myths and stories. If atheists had their way they would be a dominant force in the world, disallowing any mention of God. Fortunately we are allowed to have our own thoughts and opinions regarding things. Because of that, Christians have a standard that we attempt to follow. It gives us purpose for our lives. It gives us something outside of ourselves to turn to in our time of need. Living a life for self is an empty existence. Living for God and others is rewarding. To know this you must experience it first hand and that requires faith.

Atheists have chosen not to follow God's standard believing in their hearts that they are good. Trying is good enough in their minds. It's the other individuals who are evil, not them. They don't commit heinous crimes against humanity. I refuse to believe that they see themselves as perfect, for that seems an outrageous claim even for an atheist. I would surmise that their belief is that they are doing the best they can with the resources at their disposal and that's good enough. There's no way to know for sure because each individual in all of humanity has their own concept of what is good and evil and what we should be doing or not doing.

The point to all this is that without God there is no standard that remains consistent. Man sets the standard. He then tweaks it and molds it to make it suit his current desires or needs. Without standards there will always be power struggles. Someone always wants to be in charge. It takes place everywhere; in business, homes, churches, schools, sports teams, all walks of life. It all comes down to control; God has it, we want it. Everyone is different. Some people are passive, some aggressive; some loving and kind, others harsh and mean. The ones who seek control are pretty easy to spot. They are the ones who always have an opinion; always have a better way of doing things. An atheist's problem with this whole God thing is that they would have to relinquish control of their lives to someone they cannot see, taste, touch, smell or hear. They seem comfortable pushing their main contention, which is 'proof' or the lack thereof.

Atheism is a byproduct of free will. If it were not so there would be repercussions for unbelief. While believers contend that there will most certainly be repercussions eventually, it is not the initial issue. We live in a land where we can do as we please within the confines of the Constitution and the laws of the land. People with personal agendas have built our world. Their disbelief in a literal devil has allowed him to dangle shiny trinkets in front of people for generations. Satan has influenced the construction of a society that has developed a skewed view of life, liberty and the pursuit of happiness.

Have It Your Way

Unbelievers find 'religion' to be too restrictive in one-way or another. They want to live a 'Burger King' life … 'have it your way!' The Old Testament has a good example of how insisting on having it your own way can lead to destruction in the end. That example is found in 1 Samuel …

> "And it came about when Samuel was old that he appointed
> his sons judges over Israel. Now the name of his firstborn
> was Joel, and the name of his second, Abijah; they were
> judging in Beersheba. His sons, however, did not walk in
> his ways, but turned aside after dishonest gain and took
> bribes and perverted justice. Then all the elders of Israel

gathered together and came to Samuel at Ramah; and they said to him, "Behold, you have grown old, and your sons do not walk in your ways. Now appoint a king for us to judge us like all the nations." But the thing was displeasing in the sight of Samuel when they said, "Give us a king to judge us." And Samuel prayed to the Lord. The Lord said to Samuel, "Listen to the voice of the people in regard to all that they say to you, for they have not rejected you, but they have rejected Me from being king over them. Like all the deeds which they have done since the day that I brought them up from Egypt even to this day—in that they have forsaken Me and served other gods—so they are doing to you also. Now then, listen to their voice; however, you shall solemnly warn them and tell them of the procedure of the king who will reign over them."
(1 Samuel 8:1-9; NASB)

Samuel issued the warnings God instructed him to give the Israelites regarding having an earthly king rule over them and this was their response in verses 19-22: *"Nevertheless, the people refused to listen to the voice of Samuel, and they said, 'No, but there shall be a king over us, that we also may be like all the nations, that our king may judge us and go out before us and fight our battles.' Now after Samuel had heard all the words of the people, he repeated them in the Lord's hearing. The Lord said to Samuel, 'Listen to their voice and appoint them a king.'"*

God was to be their king that they might be different; a nation of people set apart due to their strong faith and belief in God. However, having seen the sinful ways of Samuel's sons and the fact that Samuel was very old, they seized the opportunity to make what in their eyes was a significant move to be like the other nations. This was in direct violation of God's will for them. The Old Testament chronicles the years following this critical decision. Israel had righteous, godly kings and disobedient and evil kings. All because they wanted to be like all the other nations rather than listen to Jehovah God.

They are not alone in thinking they knew better how to run their own lives without God. Down through the ages millions upon millions of people have thought the same thing. How could an unseen spirit possibly be real, let alone know what's best for them? It made no sense, so creatures that only had the capacity to utilize a small percentage of their intellect decided they knew better than the unseen spirit being who was said to have full capacity of his intellect. Atheists make one fatal mistake: they only rely on their six senses and refuse to seriously consider the existence of anything or anyone outside their realm without tangible proof. They line up with the 'seeing is believing' crowd; however, seeing is not faith and even if they *did* see God they would still find a million and one reasons not to believe. They ridicule others' belief in God stating that they are weak and in need of a crutch; all they see are people inventing a God whom they can lean on. Atheists have no intention of entertaining God's existence. Their rejection of God is a glaring error in judgment on their part. They seem content to tear down the faith of others. Their hatred and disdain for Christians leaks out, for they cannot contain it. It isn't enough to simply agree to disagree; they must eradicate all statements, insinuations and appearances of God. They attack Christmas & Easter, the two most important religious holidays on the calendar. Tearing down is selfish, destructive behavior borne out of incredible ignorance. As Christians we should strive all the more to build up and never tear down. There is a day coming when seeking God will be fruitless and all hope of forgiveness will end. Although non-believers scoff at this, we believe it is coming nonetheless. Those outside the hedge of God's protection shall feel the wrath of their rejection on that day.

Contentment

Is it just me or does it seem as though non-believers are angrier than ever about the existence of Christianity? Why is that? Is it all the perceived and actual injustice in the world that has caused them to be angry? How can God exist amid so much pain and death? God is supposed to be loving and kind, isn't He? Is it possible that atheists, along with other non-believing groups, are having difficulty finding contentment in the middle of all that exists around them? Could this be because true, lasting fulfillment and contentment can only be found in God?

True happiness isn't something one can purchase or conjure up. True happiness lies in contentment; a feeling of complete satisfaction. Perhaps contentment eludes people because they have lofty expectations for themselves that aren't going as they had planned? All our plans at best are nothing more than speculative guesses for no one can predict what will happen in the next five minutes, let alone the next day, week, month or year. We plan hoping that all will fall into line so that our plans can come to fruition; then and only then will we be content, but we never are. People pray for a winning lottery ticket thinking that becoming an instant multimillionaire will cure all their ills. Ever see those shows that air from time to time about lottery winners and how winning made their lives a living hell? Millions of dollars isn't the answer.

To Debate or Not to Debate

Okay, so we all know that atheists and Christians would make very poor bedfellows. What should Christians do? They could fight back, but should they? I have a vivid mental picture of a mob of people charging a large shield that is being held up by another group of people. Instead of trying to withstand the wave of humanity coming towards them, they wait until contact is made and then simply step aside, allowing the mob to come crashing to the ground. The mob are the atheists, the group holding up the large shield are the Christians. Fighting only makes you exhausted and takes your mind and energy off of God. Stepping aside isn't giving up, but rather allowing their force to end up being their folly. It doesn't require force to make a point; it requires a spirit of genuineness, combined with a certain level of consistency and persistence.

Perhaps debate is helpful, perhaps not. I will leave that for the theologians in the crowd to decide. My comments are for the common man; the Christian white and blue collar work-a-day Joe's and Jane's that love Christ and desire to serve Him. To them debating and arguing are fruitless endeavors. I discourage it, and 2 Timothy 2:23 is one reason why, for it says: *"Don't have anything to do with foolish and stupid arguments, because you know they produce quarrels."* This is Paul's admonition to Timothy regarding the church. So if we are to avoid such foolish and stupid arguments with the brethren, where would debates with atheists fall? Unless the Holy Spirit allows them to see the truth, they will stay in darkness. No one is outside of the reach of God's salvation; however, some simply refuse to see. The idea of a spirit being ruling and reigning over mankind is so foreign a concept to them that their ears have become deaf to the mere mention of it, their minds to the mere thought of it and their hearts have become calloused over. God knows how to reach them even when we do not. God is greater than any force known to man and doesn't wish that anyone to be lost (2 Peter 3:9). That includes atheists.

If God is real, then God loves the Atheists too. And because God loves them, I need to also. Why shouldn't I? If I am right and God either causes or allows all things, then what on earth do I have to fear from

Atheists? Psalm 118:6-7 declares *"The LORD is with me; I will not be afraid. What can mere mortals do to me? The LORD is with me; he is my helper. I look in triumph on my enemies."* I will pray for them earnestly, represent the Lord before them and see what comes of it. God is in control, not man.

I'm a proponent of knowing what you believe and why you believe it so that you can explain to those who ask about the hope you have inside. On the other hand, I'm not a proponent of endless debate with non-believers that many times end up turning contentious. I see no point to it.

Anti-theism

An anti-theist is different than an atheist in that they are opposed to belief in the existence of *any* god or gods and not merely one in particular. Anti-theism is the label given for the school of free thinkers who take the view that theism, or the belief in any god, is dangerous or destructive. Author Christopher Hitchens wrote: *"I'm not even an atheist so much as I am an anti-theist; I not only maintain that all religions are versions of the same untruth, but I hold that the influence of churches, and the effect of religious belief, is positively harmful."* Considering religious belief detrimental to society, proponents actually speak out against it, referring to themselves as evangelical atheists. Anti-theism is active opposition to theism. The term has had a range of applications; in secular contexts, it typically refers to direct opposition to organized religion or to the belief in any deity, while in a theistic context, it sometimes refers to opposition to a specific god or gods.

> *"Anti-theism requires more than either merely disbelieving in gods or even denying the existence of gods. Anti-theism requires a couple of specific and additional*

beliefs: first, that theism is harmful to the believer, harmful to society, harmful to politics, harmful to culture, etc.; second, that theism can and should be countered in order to reduce the harm it causes. If a person believes these things, then they will likely be an anti-theist who works against theism by arguing that it be abandoned, promoting alternatives, or perhaps even supporting measures to suppress it."[2]

Although anti-theism isn't new, being first mentioned back in the early 1800's, it should be considered a dangerous alternative to atheism. Loving those who hate you and all you stand for is difficult; however, it is no different than what Christ went through over 2000 years ago. Standing tall for what you believe may not always be easy; however, God is in control and will help us stand in the face of this and any opposition as we move forward declaring the goodness, mercy and forgiveness of God.

"Until my conversion in 1975 I professed to be an atheist in part because I looked at the roughly 85 percent of my fellow U.S. citizens who claimed to be Christians and could not see that their faith genuinely affected their lives. I reasoned that if even Christians did not believe in Jesus' teachings, why should I? My excuse for unbelief and the excuse of many other secularists I knew, continued until God's Spirit confronted me with the reality that the truth of Christ does not rise or fall on the claims of his professed followers, but on Jesus himself. The faith of nominal Christians may appeal to non-Christians who can use it to justify their own unbelief, but such "Christians" will have no part

in God's kingdom. Instead they will be thrown out and trampled." - Craig S. Keener [3]

———◉———

"A god who let us prove his existence would be an idol."

Dietrich Bonhoeffer

CHAPTER 3

Agnostics

A non-practicing Jewish doctor friend of mine discussed the existence of God with me on one occasion. He asked the question: "What if when your life is over you find that there is no God?" I quoted Albert Camus, French philosopher, in my reply: "I would rather live my life as if there is a God and die to find out there isn't, than live my life as if there isn't and die to find out there is." I went on to say in the end, if God didn't happen to exist, I could at the very least say I placed my faith in a standard of living that resulted in a good life. Then I faced him and said "What if God does exist? What then?" His somber reply was simply this: "I suppose I would go to hell."

In an article promoting Agnosticism, author Victor Bugliosi writes *"As far as theism is concerned, its fundamental weakness, of course, is that since no one has seen God, a belief in him has to be based on faith, since the very definition of faith is that it is a belief in something without proof. But why should we have so much faith in something for which there is no proof? And why, in so many ways, should we want to see by faith what the eye of reason rejects? We can know that the Christian God cannot exist. If he is all-powerful and all-good, as Christians maintain, there would not have been, for instance, the Holocaust. This is an inherent self- contradiction. So if Christians insist on having a God, they can do so, but if they have any respect for logic they'll have to redefine who he is. Because the Christian God cannot exist does not mean, however, that there is no God who created the universe."*[4]

Bugliosi continues in his article using the word "shatters" when referring to how he disproved the "pillars of theism" single-handedly by dismissing 'free-will', 'the virgin birth' and 'life after death' or the topic of heaven and hell as untrue and unsubstantiated. Bugliosi seems to think that he can dismiss these pillars with logic, even though earlier in his article he shows to have a clear understanding of what faith is. He goes on to ask the unanswerable question *"why should we have so much faith in something for which there is no proof? And why, in so many ways, should we want to see by faith what the eye of reason rejects?"* I consider it both presumptuous and arrogant to assume that any human logic can "shatter" the faith or beliefs of anyone.

Those that are looking for a reason not to believe will take his words and tuck them into the deep recesses of their heart for safekeeping. Their unbelief has once again been validated; however, I hardly think his words would have much effect on a well-grounded believer. Though Mr. Bugliosi feels he has proven his point, frankly I don't see that he has proven anything at all. He may have proven that faith in God is illogical, but that is not a startling revelation for the apostle Paul even admits in his first letter to the Corinthians *"For the message of the cross is foolishness to those who are perishing, but to us who are being saved it is the power of God."* (1 Corinthians 1:18) The gospel of Jesus Christ makes no logical sense whatsoever; I admit that myself. It really comes down to this simple conclusion: you either believe it or you don't. Just the fact alone that so many people research the topic of God for the purpose of disputing it might show that they want to believe in something that is greater than themselves but need experiential proof to believe. The bible clearly states in Hebrews 11:6 that unless you have faith, not evidence but *faith*, it's impossible to please God.

Agnosticism normally refers to a neutral or undecided position on the question of the existence of God. When it comes right down to it, agnostics are really nothing more than fence sitters. They aren't too sure what to believe. They don't discount God altogether, yet don't freely profess to believe in Him. Apparently they are unable to take a stand on the issue or simply not willing to.

No Proof

Seeking answers regarding why people become Agnostics, I simply asked and found the responses to be quite interesting. They included everything from a simple *"because we do not presume to know everything"* to the slightly more complex *"technically, everyone is an agnostic, because no one truly knows."* Again we go back to the same argument Atheists use: no proof. They're right. A faith based belief system isn't going to provide proof of anything. Proof negates faith and puts the topic into the realm of theory, which is fraught with human error. Christianity makes little or no sense to non-believers and without faith it never will.

Agnostics use the excuse that no one really knows the truth about the existence of God, yet that is exactly the same as saying no one really knows if George Washington was real or the figment of someone's imagination like Paul Bunyan. Sure, there are artist renderings galore, but there are of Jesus as well. No one alive today was there when Washington was alive. Perhaps all his accomplishments and heroics were made up to encourage a fledgling nation. While I don't believe that to be true, I wasn't there to prove it either way.

The thought of an unseen deity forming the sun, moon and the stars in the sky and everything in existence is a little too much for agnostics to accept. It's easier to dismiss it as a myth or fairytale then to simply embrace it as truth by faith. They believe there is something or someone out there, but it could be many gods or one. They have fallen into the same trap as the atheists. They feel the need for proof. Anything that cannot be proven logically or scientifically cannot be seriously considered to be valid and therefore is not necessarily true according to agnostics. It might be true, might not be. So they leave it up to personal interpretation. Certainly it couldn't be anything that's real and to be taken seriously. The arrogance of man only highlights his ignorance.

Faith sees through spiritual eyes the things that cannot be seen in the physical realm. It requires belief in the unseen. None of this makes sense to those who refuse to see. People are more inclined to believe in the existence of space aliens than they are in God, yet there is no concrete evidence that space aliens exist either. All they have are supposed abductions, reported sightings and blurry black and white photos that could be anything. No concrete proof exists although Roswell, NM is burgeoning with cottage businesses pushing the reality of aliens.

Because the Holy Spirit is in the business of wooing those that are lost, agnostics have a shot at redemption, in spite of themselves, just like anyone else. No one is outside the reach of God. With faith, one can receive forgiveness for their sins, enter into God's family and enjoy all He has in store for His children. To some it seems so much more sensible to lean on their own intellect and resources; however, sooner or later both will run out. Those individuals are operating on limited resources. Their intellect stems from what they've been taught. Their resources include that which they've acquired. That's it and that's all. Where can they turn when they come to the end of their rope? Those who feel hopeless get involved with some form of illegal stimulants to numb their disappointment and pain or worse, commit suicide. Without God there is no concrete basis for hope in the future. And it's all based on faith.

The Unanswerable Question

One individual's response to the question 'why do people become Agnostics?' was *"the question should be why do people STOP being agnostic and start thinking they know answers to unanswerable questions?"* Hmmm, let's look at that. The questions are unanswerable to whom? Who says there aren't any answers? It's all conjecture; an opinion or conclusion formed on the basis of incomplete information. Man, with limited intelligence, doesn't know the answer to the question regarding the existence of God, so he deems it unanswerable. Theories based on nothing but man's opinion. Agnostics are stuck really. They are caught between the proverbial rock and a hard place. They are unable to profess the existence of one solitary God who presides over all things, yet cannot bring themselves to deny His existence either.

I come across so many people in my travels that announce proudly *"oh, I believe in God"*. Perhaps our response to that should be in the form of a question ... something like: *"Great! Have you allowed Him to change your life?"* Giving lip service to God is a dangerous proposition. If people simply acknowledge the existence of God and do nothing with that discovery, why bother. God doesn't need our acceptance or acknowledgement; He desires our allegiance. In exchange God has provided a full pardon for our sinful lifestyle by virtue of Christ's death on a cross. Saying we believe in Jesus or in God or saying that we are very spiritual is meaningless if these revelations don't cause us to become a completely new person.

I find it interesting that as I read up on the subject of agnosticism I didn't find any mention of Jesus, sin, the wrath of God or the fall of man. Of course I suppose that if you're unsure of the existence of God then all other topics of like kind would be irrelevant. I believe that the key element in this discussion is God's Son, Jesus Christ. I have no doubt that there are scads of articles and books devoted to the subject of why Jesus can't be God's Son. Those who refuse to deal with the faith question end up spending endless hours attempting to refute one Christian dogma after the other. Their disbelief doesn't negate the validity of any of Christianity's main doctrines. It simply means that what can be seen with spiritual eyes shall now and forevermore remain unseen by the naked eye.

The Crux of the Matter

I think a key problem for mankind and not just Agnostics, is that many are simply ignorant of the true meaning of Christianity and what it stands for. Please realize, ignorance isn't stupidity; ignorance is simply not being aware or not having an understanding of a topic. I didn't understand what I believed about Christ or God or sin and I grew up going to church until I was 17 years old. I didn't know anything about Christ's death on the cross because either it wasn't taught or I wasn't paying attention. I didn't know about needing forgiveness for my sins because I didn't know I was a sinner … I didn't understand the concept of separation from God. Perhaps their ignorance is due to a faulty presentation of our beliefs?

Here is the crux of the matter with regards to Christianity: Jesus Christ came to earth willingly as part of God's plan to save mankind from itself. He ministered to the people, healed them of their sicknesses and diseases and even raised some from the dead. In the face of all Jesus had done, all the religious leaders could do is scoff at Him and plot to have him killed. I suppose they didn't like the competition for the Jews reverence and loyalty. The Pharisees and Sadducees, religious leaders of the day, took from the people; Christ gave. In the end, He gave Himself, which was more than anyone else could possibly give to remove the blot sin had caused on all of humanity. So when it is time to go face Almighty God before His Great White Throne, the question may well be: *"What did you do with my Jesus?"* While this question isn't documented in scripture, I can see God asking that because Christ is the linchpin to His plan of salvation. He is *the* vital piece in the puzzle known as God's Redemptive Plan for mankind. Without Christ's death on the cross there is no forgiveness for sin. Now of course, those who don't believe in God think we're off our rockers; but that's the beauty of having a free will. If they think we're nuts that's their prerogative.

The God-Conscious

> *"You believe that there is one God. Good! Even the demons believe that—and shudder."* – James 2:19

I have had associations with three different people over the last year who have all either said they believed in God or considered themselves religious or spiritual. Being spiritual can simply mean that they believe in supernatural phenomena, so I asked if that person believed in God. Judging by their extremely hedonistic lifestyle, I didn't find it to be that outlandish of a question. "Well of course I believe in God", was the reply I received. How silly of me to ask.

The other two individuals claimed to believe in God yet didn't seem to understand what I meant when I told them that Christianity isn't a religion, but rather a very personal relationship with Almighty God. They claimed to be Christians yet you wouldn't know it by the way they lived. They said they belonged to a certain denomination, which seems to be the reason they say they're Christians. They don't attend church, rarely if ever read the Bible and allow people to pray for them, but don't pray themselves. While these are all things Christians *do* and not what makes them a Christian, it would at least show some semblance of life to their faith.

I propose to you that if there's absolutely no outward evidence of a life that has been changed then we can make a safe assumption that their 'religion' involves a whole lot of talking and very little else. Based on my own past, it's very possible that they have no idea what they believe. It had become pretty obvious to me over time that they were spiritually bankrupt.

It'd be easy for someone to point an accusing finger at me and say that I am judging the above-mentioned people, but I'm not. What I *am* doing is being a fruit inspector. A fruit inspector is someone who doesn't judge a brother or sister in Christ, but simply makes observations regarding a brother or sister's spiritual growth as a means of helping them. It's not something that is discussed with others, for that would be gossip. It's done with a sense of humility, understanding that we all have flaws and rough edges that need to be smoothed. As the saying goes, *"There but for the grace of God go I."*[5]

Some folks are floundering spiritually and may appreciate a fellow Christian's assistance in getting back on track; you might consider it like getting a front-end alignment on your car. It helps you drive straight down the road rather than veer off to the left or right. Some folks want you to mind your own business and leave them alone. It's very important how the topic is broached. We are not to judge, simply attempt to bring about change based on scripture. We should be very careful. It takes a spiritually mature individual to handle this delicate situation properly. Going about it in the wrong way will only cause a divide between you and the other person.

Listen, attending a church every time the doors are open doesn't make you a Christian; it means you are an attendee. Becoming involved in a church doesn't make you a Christian either; it means you an *involved* attendee. Doing good deeds in your life is wonderful. We should all be doing good deeds for others whenever the occasion arises; but that still doesn't make you a Christian. Believing in God is all well and good, but if that's as far as it goes than you're short changing yourself in a big way. Receiving God's forgiveness through Christ's death on the cross and entering into a personal relationship with Him is what makes you a Christian. Striving to become more like Christ each day makes you an *obedient* Christian.

Believing vs. Knowing

Let me say a little on the difference between believing and knowing. Believing in something or someone can mean one of two things. It can mean that you have accepted something as true or it can mean to have a firm (unwavering) religious faith. Knowing what I know about the individuals I mention just before, I can tell that they believe God exists but have thus far not gotten to the point where they have placed their unwavering trust in Him for all things. To 'know' something or someone in the Biblical sense is to have intimate knowledge of them. This is how God knows us. We strive to know Him in like manner. So you can see that there is a world of difference between simply believing and knowing something or someone, at least in the biblical sense of the word.

Dabblers

Some individuals are what I refer to as 'dabblers'. They feed their mind with books and television shows on psychic phenomenon, witchcraft, demonic possession and paranormal activity in a rather casual way. They either claim it's simply so they can understand it or that they find it entertaining. I told one individual who professed to be a Christian that he needed to be very careful what he fed into his mind. He, in turn, insisted that it was nothing more than harmless fun. I told him he was foolish for messing with such things. He smirked at me; his arrogance regarding the matter was obvious. Apparently, I just didn't understand. There are no doubt many others who feel that where they go and what they listen to, read or watch will have no ill effects on them because it's all being done in good fun. The fact is their belief in God will do *nothing* for them unless they activate it and to activate it is to plug into the Holy Spirit and fill yourself with God, *not* other peripheral and I might add, non-essential things that hold no eternal value. Hopefully they will come to their senses before it's too late. While doing the right thing is never wrong, doing the wrong thing is never, ever right. I consider it wrong to fill your mind with evil no matter how innocently it may be presented. Always remember Paul's response to the spiritually arrogant Corinthians; yes, you can do as you please, but not all things are beneficial or constructive.

Spiritual Dehydration

I lived in Texas for nine years and experienced some of the hottest weather I've ever had to endure. I have never been a big fan of heat, so summers were always a challenge for me. When I ventured out to cut my lawn for the first time in the heat of the day I lasted about 15 minutes before I started to have what I refer to as 'white-outs'. I was slowly becoming dehydrated and didn't even realize it. Instead of just going into the air conditioning and calling it a day, I drank water and Gatorade until I thought I would burst to rehydrate my system. Even with constant hydration I still needed to stop and sit for a little while a few times. It was brutal.

If you say you believe in God yet don't enter into the relationship He desires to have with you, you will become spiritually dehydrated and not even realize it. To ignore God's word and just give Him lip service instead of partaking is like allowing yourself to starve while sitting at a banqueting table filled with food. It amazes me how foolish and close-minded some folks are. They proclaim their beliefs yet live life as they choose. They are nothing more than rudderless ships.

As believers, we haven't been given the option to give God a head nod as we go on by. While it's true we can live our lives as we want, consequences always follow. God requires faith and submission, not simply acknowledgement. He doesn't need us to believe in Him alone, but to immerse ourselves in all that He is. I think many people are afraid they will be perceived as 'Jesus freaks' or 'Holy rollers' if they get too involved with God or become too vocal regarding their faith. That isn't the point at all. It's not what we say as much as what we do and how we live that will speak to people, not proclaiming our faith loudly to passersby. That is not to say that we enter heaven by virtue of our deeds, it's just that what we do in the name of the Lord is the only thing non-believers can experience from us that will have a positive influence. Words might touch a cord, but back them up with action and you've really hit the mark.

Evangelism by Force

God loves the unsaved and certainly hasn't forgotten them; however, the way some Christians act towards unbelievers you wouldn't know it. Judgment rather than mercy and grace seem to be the weapon of choice to bludgeon their victims with. Revelation 3:20 depicts Christ knocking on the door asking for entrance (symbolic of Him asking to come into our hearts and as a result, our lives). It seems some would rather kick the door in like the Huns of old, plundering as they go. Is it any wonder some folks have such disdain for Christians? Based on the words and actions of some of the Christians I've encountered throughout my adult life, if I didn't know better, I wouldn't want to become a Christian either. We shouldn't force our way into people's lives in an effort to bring them to Christ. We may find one out of a hundred who needs a heavy hand but that shouldn't be our normal approach.

Our mission was His mission; to save the lost. How did Jesus approach sinners? God does the saving; we are merely conduits. We are not judge and jury, He is. Shunning people because they are sinners' flies directly in the face of what Christ was doing and what God is trying to do today. We aren't being asked to approve of their lifestyle, we are being asked to show them the same loving mercy and compassion we were shown by God.

I want to share a real life illustration to a saying that I'm sure you are all familiar with: 'You can lead a horse to water, but you can't make him drink.' This took on new meaning for me when my first wife bought some property with her sister and subsequently bought some horses to ride. One Saturday my youngest daughter and I were playing around with one of the horses. She brought the horse over to the water trough for him to take a drink. He just stood there. She then took his muzzle and gently pushed it into the cool water. He abruptly jerked his head back and trotted away. We led that horse to the water, but even after his muzzle was pushed down into the water he refused to drink. That's the way it is with non-believers. Nothing we could ever say or do will make a difference if they are not open to what we are saying. The Holy Spirit woos, but if they are not of a mind to even consider what you are presenting to them, then the door is closed, the lights are out and nobody is home. Perhaps a seed is being planted, only God would know that, so we are not to cease presenting the gospel when an opportunity arises, but for goodness sake, use compassion and a modicum of discretion. We should never shove the gospel down anyone's throat. It won't taste very good and they will resent you for it.

God Did it

There are people who find fault with God for things He has done in history and justify their disbelief or hesitancy to believe due to such actions. One such example is the killing of animals as sacrificial offerings. In essence they are placing the life of a creature over their trust and belief in the creator of that creature; although they don't see it that way, of course. They only see all animals as precious and they cannot accept the fact that a loving God would kill an innocent animal for no apparent reason. Nothing could be further from the truth. There is a very specific reason for their death. It's imperative that the whole picture is taken into consideration. God created animals to be beasts of burden and food for man, not necessarily to be their pets. Dogs, cats, bunnies, ferrets and hamsters (to arbitrarily name a few) were not slaughtered to redeem the Jews of the Old Testament. It was bulls, goats, lambs or calves that were sacrificed. That is no doubt bad enough for those who love all animals; however, these animals were a vital part of God's sacrificial system prior to Christ's coming. In God's redemptive system blood was the payment required to cover a person's sin. I understand people's love for animals, but they are missing the point of their own sinfulness. Sadly, in large part, they don't even want to discuss it.

Back in the mid-1980's I encountered an elderly woman who loved animals. I wanted to speak with her about heaven and God and she cut me off saying that any God that killed innocent animals wasn't a God she wanted to have anything to do with. I thanked her for her time and left quietly. You cannot make people believe in God. Even God doesn't want followers based on restrictive requirements, but rather willing submission.

There are people who blame God for the damages and deaths caused from forces of nature; e.g., hurricanes, tornadoes, tsunamis, earthquakes, etc. Some folks seem to think it has to be someone's fault. It's almost like combining the blame game with pin the tail on the donkey. Who shall we blame today? Again, a lack of understanding regarding who God is and what He does and doesn't do is in play here. Some people simply have a bone to pick with someone and it might as well be God. How could He do such a thing; all the needless death and devastation has to be someone's fault. When all else fails, blame God; God did it.

Making a Difference

In light of all the pain and tragedy that comes with living life in this day and age we can't force people to see things our way. Those we are trying to win for Christ will dig in their heels and nothing we could ever say would make any difference. We must allow God to slowly mold us into the type of person that is real. People will listen to someone they feel is genuine. Do you want to make a difference in this sin sick world? Let God make the necessary alterations from the inside out so that you can be that consistently genuine believer who doesn't cheapen the grace of God, but rather lives it out right in front of the world he is attempting to change.

"A man can no more diminish God's glory by refusing to worship Him than a lunatic can put out the sun by scribbling the word, 'darkness' on the walls of his cell."

C. S. Lewis

CHAPTER 4

APOSTATES

I recently heard about a Baptist minister who renounced his faith in God stating that he now considered himself a bona fide atheist. He no longer believed in the existence of God, nor did he believe the Bible was God's inerrant word. He cited the following encounter as the reason for his renunciation. A man he knew had a young wife who had cancer. The man begged and pleaded with God to heal her, however, the woman died. The minister had no words of comfort for this man, but rather became angry. He could no longer believe in a God who would apparently ignore the pleadings of a husband for the life of his wife to be spared.

The Big Picture

> "And I heard a loud voice from the throne saying, 'Look! God's dwelling place is now among the people, and he will dwell with them. They will be his people, and God himself will be with them and be their God.' 'He will wipe every tear from their eyes. There will be no more death' or mourning or crying or pain, for the old order of things has passed away.'"
> (Revelation 21:3-4)

The Apostle John, writer of Revelations, took these verses from Isaiah 25:8. So when a Christian who dies from an illness passes on to heaven they receive the final healing he or she will ever need. The Baptist minister who renounced his faith over such an incident was rather shortsighted. Naturally the husband wanted his wife back. There was no mention of it, but there may have been children involved too. The minister apparently couldn't stand to see someone so young in so much distress. The minister couldn't see the bigger picture. He needed to look at things from God's perspective.

When a person is terminally ill and we earnestly pray for a physical healing, there are times when they are healed and remain with us on the earth. If a person is healed, they can theoretically contract the same illness again at a later date. There are also times we must consider the fact that the healing the individual receives may involve their dying. In cases such as these our prayers for healing are answered in a more complete and irreversible way. It is a normal selfish response to want the dying person to be with us, but whether someone believes in God or not, everyone dies at some point in life. God alone knows what pain and heartache He may have saved the deceased individual and their loved ones from in the future had they lived. We all must remember that when someone we have prayed for dies, according to scripture they shall never be sick again.

The Apostasy

> "Now the Spirit expressly says that in later times some will depart from the faith by devoting themselves to deceitful spirits and teachings of demons, through the insincerity of liars whose consciences are seared, who forbid marriage and require abstinence from foods that God created to be received with thanksgiving by those who believe and know the truth."
> (1 Timothy 4:1-3; ESV)

Scripture is clear that some *will* fall away from the faith. Why do people renounce God? Generally speaking people walk away from their faith in God because they have allowed other things to crowd Him out of their lives. He is no longer the focus of their life, but rather an afterthought that soon becomes no thought at all. False teachings that have familiar elements of God in it woo those who are not spiritually knowledgeable. Other 'religions' or cults soft peddle sin by declaring things considered sinful by Christian standards to *not* be sinful after all. In the face of trials, destruction, disappointment and death people lose sight of what faith truly is. Their vision is blurred and that causes their standards to become skewed.

Someone who becomes a Christian only to spiritually starve themselves will likely end up falling away from God. Such an individual has reaped the benefit of salvation, namely forgiveness, never realizing there was more to it. Spiritual laziness can cause believers to fall away from the faith due to a lack of growth. With your physical body, if you don't eat properly and keep yourself hydrated, you will become sick. This can happen spiritually as well. If you don't feed your spirit man you will become sick in that area of your life as well. You are ripe for falling away from God. Not realizing the importance of maintaining your spiritual walk with God, you squander opportunities to bless others and glorify God, choosing instead self- gratification. Compromising your beliefs will only satisfy the dying part of you.

I knew a brother that I attended Bible School with back in the 80's who graduated and became head Pastor of a small church in Illinois. He struggled with the congregation's lack of zeal and willingness to assist with ministries within the church. My friend ended up at some point renouncing his faith in Christ. I don't know all the nuances of his decision; however, several years ago I found him on face book and we stayed connected for a short time. He sent me a lengthy thesis he had written on why God didn't exist and pointed me towards numerous books written by men who were atheists. I was not only shocked but also disappointed. I believe that some people are too smart for their own good. My friend was very intelligent but all his research ended up being his downfall for he wasted his time studying things that turned him away from God. Listen to 2 Peter 2:20 … *"For if, after they have escaped the defilements of the world through the knowledge of our Lord and Savior Jesus Christ, they are again entangled in them and overcome, the last state has become worse for them than the first."* Regardless of whether a person lives a good life by the world's standards or a life filled with evil deeds, they have still turned away from the one true standard which the creator of the universe established.

Back-Sliders

There is an estimated 200 verses throughout the Bible that deal with the topic of those who have fallen away from the faith. In evangelical circles those people can be said to have 'back-slidden' away from God. They no longer go to church, no longer pray, no longer read their Bible and no longer seek the wisdom of God for their life decisions. They have not publically renounced God or consciously turned their back on Him; they have rather become complacent and begun doing that which they did prior to their conversion. They are still loved by God and still forgiven; however, they are in danger of reaching a point of no return. Whether it was peer pressure or a lack of understanding, the backslider carries a sense of guilt all the while justifying in their own mind the backward steps they have taken. Judging or rebuking these folks isn't advised because it typically will drive them further away from where they once were with the Lord. Compassion and mercy needs to be extended to help them see and understand that Christianity is a personal relationship with Almighty God and they have taken a hiatus from the relationship. At times some folks need to fall backwards temporarily before they can return with renewed fire. God allows this because He knows it is necessary for them to go through certain experiences. These experiences become lessons that are designed to draw them back into a right relationship with their God.

It is imperative to look at how Jesus dealt with various types of people. Never did He rebuke non-believers; He instructed through parables that people could relate to and understand. We cannot know the true motivation of a man for God alone knows a man's heart. (1 Samuel 16:7) He alone knows the true reasons for their departure from the faith. God allows it because He is not a dictator or tyrant that demands allegiance. It is our choice to serve or not to serve. Those that serve God do so willingly.

Some folks choose not to believe in God after they have followed Him for a time because they grew up in it and it has become stale to them. They were pew babies, bouncing on their mother's knee during service every time the doors were open. Once they reached the age of responsibility and went off to college they decided for themselves that they had been missing out on a whole passel of fun. This isn't the same as renouncing your faith; it falls under the Prodigal Son (or Daughter) category (Luke 15:11-32). They take part in all the world has to offer only to find, sometimes years later, that all the promises made about fun and satisfaction were wrong. I know for I was guilty of this very thing, although, my situation was somewhat different. I grew up in a church that didn't preach the gospel, per se. Their feel good message went in one ear and out the other and as a result left me empty inside. It wasn't until I gave my life to Christ that I realized this.

God Shaped Hole

I believe God made us with a place deep within our core. The only thing that will fit in that place is the Holy Spirit. I can't prove that, I just believe it to be so because I was like a rudderless ship prior to Christ coming into my life and now I have a purpose and feel the presence of God's Spirit in me. It's His essence that resides within the soul of every believer. When that place remains empty, there comes a longing for something to fill it. We don't know what that thing is so in our finite wisdom we try to stuff all sorts of things in that place only to find out that nothing else fits. No matter what we try satisfaction and fulfillment escape us. Like a wild horse that needs to be tamed, we buck wildly in an effort to resist a saddle being put on us. We don't want to conform. We don't want to follow a standard. We'd rather set our own standard. I believe that to be true of everyone. We all want some semblance of control. No one is going to tell us how to live our lives; so many simply dismiss the notion that some supreme spirit being rules over all things. The ridiculous part of all this is that we all follow a standard that has been set up by someone other than ourselves whether we realize it or not. There are laws. Break a law and there are consequences. If you live in the United States and collect a paycheck you are required by law to pay your taxes to the government by April 15th each year. If you don't there are consequences. If you reject Christ, choosing to live for yourself there are consequences then too.

The Fallen

2 Peter 2:20-22, shown earlier in the chapter, tells of those who escaped the defilements of the world only to become entangled and overcome by them once again. The Bible says that those individuals

would have been better off never having known the grace and mercy of God in the first place, for their standing is far worse now than if they had never known God to begin with. And yet those who walk away from God aren't thinking about anything but what they are walking towards. They have talked themselves or have had someone else talk them into believing that their faith in God was not real or perhaps even that God doesn't exist at all. Knowing what we believe and why we believe it is incredibly important, for it will help keep you from swaying to and fro spiritually speaking. If God is the focal point of your life then you are less likely to fall away from Him. Focusing on Almighty God, rather than those things that surround us, makes us strong in our faith. Reliance on God is solidified based on our unwavering belief that He *is* and that He rewards those whose faith is in Him.

Luke 8:13 is from the Parable of the Sower. The seeds that have no root blow away. As soon as testing comes to some in the form of trials and tribulations, they walk away. I suppose there may be many who were expecting a nirvana-like existence where they would never experience any difficulty, disappointment or pain. The fact of the matter is that the life of a believer is chocked full of trouble. The difference is that we turn to God to see what we are to learn from our trials rather than complain. Okay, maybe we complain, even whine a bit until we grow up spiritually and mature, learning over time that there are lessons to be learned from each situation we find ourselves in. God doesn't waste life experiences without teaching us something of eternal value. I have walked with the Lord over 34 years and I am still learning lessons. We stop learning the day we pass from this world into the next or at least that's the way it should be. The person who thinks they know it all is a sad person because they are closed minded to new things God may want to show them. Open your mind and heart to what God wants to tell you.

———◆———

"Nothing in the world is more dangerous than sincere ignorance and conscientious stupidity."

Martin Luther King, Jr.

CHAPTER 5

HEDONISTS

In seeking the depths of the Internet for examples of hedonistic behavior, I came upon a blog written by a family man whom for privacy purposes we shall refer to as Tom. He appears to be at the very least God conscience in that across his blog he has the words PRAY HARD – WORK HARD – TRUST GOD. I think it's a safe assumption the man isn't an atheist. He wrote an interesting entry regarding hedonism based on his observations while in Las Vegas. The following is part of his entry:

> "For the past four or five days I have been in Las Vegas working a convention. Hedonism professes that happiness is the equal to physical pleasure and also the possession of things that bring us pleasure. I sat and did a little people watching to view people and their actions and the only explanation I could muster up to justify their actions was that they were acting on their hedonistic tendencies and enjoying the pleasures that they have so rightly earned and so deeply feel the urge and need to experience.
>
> Two events of particular exclusivity in Las Vegas stuck out to me like a sore thumb. Gambling and prostitution are two of the most hedonistic activities available for pleasure in Vegas. The slogan of "What Happens in Vegas, Stays in Vegas" is very similar to the slogan for Hedonistic view

of Carpe Diem or "Seize the Day." In other words, live it up. I remember reading that hedonistic people believe that all pleasure is automatically good. That would be the only reason I could actually believe. That someone would be willing to throw outrageous amount of money away in a casino that you fully understand is not in the business of losing money and to also throw away your dignity and self-respect for the flesh of a prostitute or stripper to enjoy for a hedonistic moment of pleasure; because all pleasure is automatically good."

Pursuing pleasure to the exclusion of all else. Indulging in whatever seems right and brings one pleasure. Indulgence is the name of the game while discretion remains home on the shelf. In Buddhism, as we shall see in chapter 8, pleasure minus pain is deemed as the highest form of good; a nirvana-like existence, although I don't think gambling and prostitution is what they had in mind. Since pain is unavoidable in life, it would appear that the hedonist must avoid circumstances that will inflict pain on them. The hedonist becomes immersed in the philosophy of self-satisfaction; they are only concerned with their own pleasure and not the pleasure of others; impulse overtakes self-control.

Self-Control

"A man without self-control is like a city broken into and left without walls." (Proverbs 25:28; ESV)

Solomon paints a vivid verbal picture in the verse above, which states that a man without self-control has no established boundaries. Once boundaries are removed, standards are broken down and trouble is inevitable. Man is incapable of fending off temptations forever and will inevitably succumb to them.

Once a man is forgiven by God they are to turn away from hedonistic practices and cultivate that which is pleasing to God in their lives. The Fruit of the Spirit are character traits that every believer should seek and exhibit. They are all listed below; self-control is one of them.

> "But the fruit of the Spirit is love, joy, peace, patience, kindness, goodness, faithfulness, gentleness, self-control; against such things there is no law." (Galatians 5:22-23; ESV)

Discussion of the Fruit of the Spirit is for another book, however, I would like to look a little closer at self-control. Can a person develop self-control outside of God? It would seem to me that anyone through sheer will and determination could become a self-controlled individual. That takes discipline. Some have a lack of discipline in certain areas of their lives and yet are highly disciplined in others. If we tap into the Spirit of God and allow Him to lead and guide us into all truth, then those of us who are not as disciplined in the spiritual aspects of Godly living will have a better chance of succeeding. The only way we can achieve a disciplined spiritual life is to cultivate an intimate relationship with our God. That takes time, effort and perseverance. We must determine in our heart that we will draw close to God for it is through Him that everything true, fulfilling and lasting is found.

> "His divine power has given us everything we need for a godly life through our knowledge of him who called us by his own glory and goodness. Through these he has given us his very great and precious promises, so that through them

you may participate in the divine nature, having escaped the corruption in the world caused by evil desires. For this very reason, make every effort to add to your faith goodness; and to goodness, knowledge; and to knowledge, self-control; and to self-control, perseverance; and to perseverance, godliness; and to godliness, mutual affection; and to mutual affection, love. For if you possess these qualities in increasing measure, they will keep you from being ineffective and unproductive in your knowledge of our Lord Jesus Christ. But if any of you do not have them, you are nearsighted and blind, and you have forgotten that you have been cleansed from your past sins." (2 Peter 1:3-9)

Peter tells us up above what will happen if we possess these qualities in increasing measure: it will keep us from "being ineffective and unproductive in our knowledge of Christ". As we grow in the grace and knowledge of our Lord we will slowly become more and more like Him. If we do not have these characteristics, Peter tells us very pointedly that we are "nearsighted and blind and have forgotten that we have been cleansed from our past sins".

Seeing Others as God Sees Us

In Chapter 1, we saw in 1 Corinthians 10:23 that we are able to do as we please; however, not everything that we do is beneficial or constructive. We cannot get away from the consequences that follow our words, actions or reactions. Self-control is needed for our own benefit so that we do not overextend ourselves and become lost in the process. As Christians we mustn't veer off course. God has a path set for us to follow. Sadly, the rabbit trails we often find ourselves on lead us nowhere but away from God. Pleasure in and of itself is not wrong; however, the pursuit of it to the exclusive of all else reveals a lack of discipline.

Those that focus on pleasure, excluding God from the equation, are essentially on their own and will be subject to the winds and waves of circumstance that buffet each of us. Captivated by a sense of infallibility, they fail to realize how incredibly flawed we all truly are. Those who know Christ and stray have lost their spiritual focus and are no longer listening to God's Spirit for guidance or direction. Believers need to realize that the only difference between the world and us is that we are forgiven; there is essentially no other difference at our core. With this in mind it seems incredible how quickly Christians lose sight of their own inadequacies. The odd thing is that we are always so quick to point out the failings of others. It seems to me we're all trying to compensate for our own shortcomings by throwing a spotlight on *anyone* else's. We are not liked at all by non-believers many times because we are inconsistent and unyielding. We need to remember from whence we came. Look at others, whether Christian or not, through the eyes of God and also take a very hard look at ourselves in the mirror while we're at it. Mirrors don't lie; they show every wart, scar and blemish. No amount of makeup can remove them; it only provides an attractive facade. God overlooks our blemishes. We must learn to do the same regarding the blemishes in others.

The Golden Rule

> *"So in everything, do to others what you would have them do to you, for this sums up the Law and the Prophets."*
> (Matthew 7:12)

I have tried so hard to live this verse of scripture each day. At times I'm successful, other times not so much. I'm flawed. I know it and so does

God. I seek to be like Christ daily; however, consistently fall far short of my goal. To quote "Dirty Harry" Callahan of cinematic fame: *"A man needs to know his limitations."*[6] I know mine all too well. I'm trusting God that someday I will line up more cleanly with His will for me and shed some of these faults. Until then I will keep moving forward and thank Him for His mercy, patience and grace.

Have you ever thought of what the world would be like if we all treated others the way we wanted to be treated. This world would be shockingly different. One of the major obstacles that keep it from happening is our propensity to judge others by their outward appearance or the way they act. I'm not just talking about non-believers; I'm talking about everyone. We look at others with a jaundiced eye and make an instant assessment based on the clothes they wear, the way they carry themselves, how they talk or how they act. Did God make that assessment of us when we came to Him for forgiveness? No way. Who are we to make such an assessment? Beats me, but we pretty much all do it. I know I do and I'm not proud of that one little bit.

In light of all our faults and failings, how can we possibly make any kind of impact on this corrupt and dying world in which we live? Part of God's plan is that His children go about planting seeds of redemption in the hearts of men. Success lies in our being genuine and consistent. We need to begin to see others the way God sees them no matter who they are, what they may look like or what they may have done. God didn't pass judgment on us, although He could have. We need to see non-believers for what they are – souls in need of forgiveness. God has created each one of us and therefore loves each one of us equally. *We* were accepted just as we are, warts and all, without hesitation by Almighty God. Our acceptance by God is because He loves us. He loves us because He created us. Christ's crucifixion is evidence of His deep, abiding and everlasting love for His children. We are to love others in like manner.

"Those who belong to Christ Jesus have crucified the sinful nature with its passions and desires." (Galatians 5:24)

The crucifixion of Christ illustrates what has happened to our old sinful nature once we receive redemption resulting in the forgiveness of our sins. Essentially, it is nailed to the cross with Christ. Unfortunately we may find that it will come down off the cross and influence us again and again in our walk with God and that's not a good thing. Perhaps if we fully realized the impact and reality of the above verse we would begin to understand that our sinful nature doesn't *have* to rise up and take control ever again. In our humanity we stumble when we should be climbing to the next higher level in our spiritual growth. We are tested and found wanting with regards to our dedication and end up turning left when we ought to turn right. Once off the cross our sinful nature raises its ugly head at the worst possible moment to try to take us down. This tends to happen to strong believers, as they are much more of a threat to the enemy then passive believers. The closer we stay to God the easier we will be able to ward off such attacks.

Submission

"Submit yourselves, then, to God. Resist the devil, and he will flee from you. Come near to God and he will come near to you." (James 4:7-8a)

Submitting is yielding. We are being told to yield to God. He is all seeing, all knowing, all-powerful and all places at one time by His Spirit. That trumps anything this world can offer. Resisting is either "withstanding the effect of" or "ignoring the attraction of", in this case the devil. We cannot defeat temptation on our own; we'll lose every time. God's desire is that we become so close to Him that we can stare the devil in the eye and not blink. Satan is a defeated foe. That makes him very dangerous. Why? He has absolutely nothing to lose. He will pull out all the stops to trip us up and make us ineffective for God. He can't do that unless we give him a foothold in our lives. Ephesians 4:27 tells us not to provide an opening for Satan to influence us in any way (hence my warning to dabblers in the last chapter). There is nothing he can do to us unless God allows it; however, in our own disobedience, we can circumvent God's immediate plans for us by allowing the devil to have his way in our lives even for a moment. Consequences result from that disobedience. While God can and does provide a way of escape, we need to want it, seek it and seize it. God doesn't force Himself on anyone. We can stay in our own self-constructed 'happy place'; however, sooner or later we will come to find that we are in the wrong place. It's our responsibility to realize this. The Holy Spirit will work at getting our attention, but we can switch off our sensitivity to Him quite easily. Focus on those things around us rather than God and we will be like a ship lost at sea. We're going somewhere, but have no idea where. Eventually the current will take us where it will and only then will we come to find that it's not at all where we intended to go. God is there to take us back anytime we get around to seeking Him again. The time wasted with trivialities is irretrievable. Regret is our only consolation and so it must be, for without regret we would be prone to charting the same errant path all over again at some future date.

Yielding to God ties in to the whole faith/trust package that we put into action when we first receive Christ into our hearts and lives. What does a Yield Sign on the roadways do? It tells us to allow those on an intersecting road the right of way. Yielding is allowing God to have the right of way in our lives. Since God is said to be perfect and without flaw, we need to quickly come to the realization that we are lacking in every way. The only way non-believers can deal with such a statement is to glibly deny His existence, thus elevating their stature in their own minds.

Hedonists see nothing wrong with their behavior, citing the notion that they are only doing what pleases them and in the process not harming anyone else. As a result, they misunderstand who God is and underestimate the result of separation from Him. They are ignorant to what sin truly is and what its effect on them will be in the end. As Christians, we misrepresent God by passing judgment on them when it is their actions that are distasteful to God, not them as individuals. We are to live the life of Christ and strive to show people their own sin in a manner than doesn't single them out or ridicule them. There ought to be something about us as believers that draw others to us; that something is the Holy Spirit of God. We have nothing to offer anyone in and of ourselves. It's the Holy Spirit who resides within us that offers everything anyone would ever need this side of heaven; starting with redemption.

God doesn't walk around with a huge sledgehammer looking to slam those who are living in disobedience and we shouldn't either. He saved each of us exactly where we are, as we are. We didn't have to clean ourselves up. So why do we treat unbelievers differently then God treated us? We must seek to be filled to overflowing with God's mercy and grace and the knowledge to dispense it effectively; namely, in a manner than glorifies God and draws unbelievers to Christ. God knows exactly how to accomplish this. We only think we know, but apparently we're way off base. People ought to be drawn to us, but instead our "I'm right, you're wrong" attitude has driven them away. Submit to God and yield to the Spirit daily.

———◦———

"Desires dictate our priorities, priorities shape our choices, and choices determine our actions."
Dallin H. Oaks

CHAPTER 6

HOMOSEXUALITY

A hot button topic to be sure, homosexuality has leaked into the church. Many who have felt shunned by Christians in the past are feeling very much at home in some orthodox denominational churches. There are now entire homosexual congregations. It's a hot button because there are still huge numbers of believers who refuse to accept them *period*, let alone accept them into the mainstream of Christendom. Why would homosexuals feel their lifestyle is acceptable in the sight of God? Perhaps this article found on www.gaychurch.org may shed some light on this question.

"John 3:16 'For God so loved the world that He gave His one and only Son, that whoever believes in Him shall not perish but have eternal life.' The simplicity of the truth hit me. I had been asking the wrong6question! The issue was not sin, but salvation! God had told us that "whosoever" (King James translation) believes in Him would not perish. "Whosoever" did not exclude anyone, instead it included everyone! There was simply no group of people who would, or could, be excluded from God's salvation. It did not matter what sin you committed, if you were gay or straight, black or white, male or female. None of it made a difference. What mattered was whether you believed in Jesus Christ or not and had accepted Him as your savior! It was that simple. I sensed the Holy Spirit telling me to study salvation, not sin, for my questions would be answered there."[7]

The writer of this article has essentially manipulated scripture by omission in that they have ignored other scriptures condemning their lifestyle all the while embracing the general truth that God loves us all and awards eternal life to those who believe in Him. In this case, they did so by ignoring Leviticus 18:22 from the Old Testament and 1 Timothy 1:8-11 from the New Testament which are both listed below. Though I believe the writer is sincere and the omission hasn't been done intentionally, it is still manipulation by omission.

> "*Therefore, if anyone is in Christ, he is a new creation; old things have passed away; behold, all things have become new.*" (2 Corinthians 5:17; NKJV)

> "*You were taught, with regard to your former way of life, to put off your old self, which is being corrupted by its deceitful desires; to be made new in the attitude of your minds; and to put on the new self, created to be like God in true righteousness and holiness.*" (Ephesians 4:22-24)

We all have a sin debt that we are born with. When we receive God's forgiveness as provided by Christ's death, we are to remove our old nature as if it were a set of filthy clothes. We are then to put on our new life. The Holy Spirit would never have told anyone that they should focus on salvation, disregarding their sin, for salvation is the removal of our sins. That would make God - the Holy Spirit at odds with God - the Father and God - the Son, thus creating a division within the Trinity. That's impossible for if it were true it would cause the entirety of Christian belief system to topple. Since God is no respecter of persons, what is required of me is required of a homosexual.

If a homosexual person truly receives Christ into his heart and has their sins purged from them, there is supposed to be a death that occurs; that being the death of their old nature; part of that old nature would be their homosexual tendencies. To declare that gays can be a part of God's family and still practice sin is a major contradiction that is born out of the practice of reading into the scripture your own interpretation or ideas.

The article's author is both right and wrong in their assessment of John 3:16. Yes, no matter who you are or what you've done you can approach God and have your sins forgiven. No matter what you may have done you are loved and once forgiven, accepted by God; but there's more to it than that. While it's true that God loves all of His creation, He will never accept sin into heaven. If a person receives Christ yet doesn't allow the Holy Spirit to change them, what have they truly gained? You can't have it both ways; forgiveness and living in sin doesn't mesh. I had been perplexed as to how gays could say they loved Christ, yet still live in sin but now that I have looked into it, I see that they have apparently fooled themselves into thinking they can live as they choose without consequences. Going against God's word will bring dire consequences, no matter how many scriptures you use to defend your position. We are to rightly divide the word of God, not twist it to mean what we want it to so we can justify our lifestyle. It simply doesn't work that way.

The Bible is very clear regarding relations with the same sex. Both the Old and the New Testament weigh in on the topic:

> "Do not have sexual relations with a man as one does with a woman; that is detestable." (Leviticus 18:22)

> "We know that the law is good if one uses it properly. We also know that the law is made not for the righteous but for lawbreakers and rebels, the ungodly and sinful, the unholy

and irreligious, for those who kill their fathers or mothers, for murderers, for the sexually immoral, for those practicing homosexuality, for slave traders and liars and perjurers— and for whatever else is contrary to the sound doctrine that conforms to the gospel concerning the glory of the blessed God, which he entrusted to me." (1Timothy 1:8-11)

There is no indication anywhere in scripture that these commands are no longer in force. It's disappointing to me that the writer of the above article could have missed the mark so completely with their shift in focus off sin and onto salvation. It is a dangerous thing when someone invokes the name of the Holy Spirit as the One revealing a certain thought or instruction, especially when the sin is clearly dealt with in scripture. The Holy Spirit, as part of the Holy Trinity, never contradicts Jehovah God or His word.

The Irreverent Reverend

In my local newspaper recently there appeared a headline for an editorial piece that read "THE LAW LAGS, BUT GOD BLESSES SAME-SEX UNIONS".[8] The writer was a local minister who has taken the pen name 'The Irreverent Reverend'. He says Christians who are opposed to same-sex marriage don't know their *"halo from their hip bone"*. He claims that those in opposition are clinging *"to the half dozen or so verses that condemn homosexuality like a guy clinging to a life preserver in the riptide of history. You're drowning, so you don't care about history, science or context."* Let's analyze his bold proclamation. Take history; where in history was it alright for followers of God to enter into relationship with the same sex? The answer is 'nowhere', to the best of my knowledge. Let's take science; the writer claims, *"the miracle of marriage shouldn't be reduced to mere anatomy".* Genesis 2:20-25 doesn't have God taking another man from Adam's side, but a woman to be his helpmate and wife. Where did this whole idea of same-sex marriage come from because it doesn't appear to have come from God? Have we taken the condemning verses of scripture out of context to make our case against homosexuality as a lifestyle? I don't believe that is the case at all. In Genesis, there is no mention of same-sex unions. Throughout scripture there is nothing positive said about same-sex anything. There is actually no context to misrepresent, for it appears in no context at all except where it is declared in scripture as sinful. When God speaks regarding things of importance He is very clear about what He is saying and doesn't leave a whole lot to interpretation.

The writer goes on to mention how Kings in the Old Testament had concubines or multiple wives which is undoubtedly how he is tying historical practices to same-sex relationships. Kings, such as David, had many wives. At this time in history it apparently wasn't a sinful practice. If you look long and hard enough you can find text to support just about anything you choose to believe; however, this doesn't validate same-sex marriage.

Indeed, it would appear that the writer of this piece is focusing on what he feels is an apparent injustice rather than what the Bible truly says. If God really loves all of His creation then why would He condemn a portion of it just for falling in love? One could ask the same question regarding adultery. If God really loves His creation then why is it wrong for a man or women bound by marriage yet no longer having feelings for one another, to 'carry on' with someone else whom they have 'fallen deeply in love with' while still married? God has set a standard of right and wrong; they are the Ten Commandments. They stood as the one standard to live by until Christ fulfilled them with His death. Although the Mosaic Law no longer binds us, our new life in Christ should be such that we would naturally live them out even though we are no longer required to. Having accepted God's gift of forgiveness by faith we are to be pleasing to God in our thoughts, words and deeds as directed and enabled by the Holy Spirit. With scripture as our guide we would do much better to err on the side of caution when we are unsure then to reinterpret verses to suit our situation or our feelings at the time.

Fortunately this individual hasn't said that the Holy Spirit revealed this to him. No, this came from his own dissection of the Bible. In the end, God will sort all things out. If this writer is that positive that God can and does "bless a union between two men or two women", I sure hope he's right. However, I see no biblical evidence that he is.

The Sin Not the Sinner

In light of the hatred that this topic has spawned, it should be pointed out that nowhere in the Bible does it say that God hates any one type of person. What it says is that He hates the things they do. God does not hate homosexuals; however, their lifestyle is a contradiction to what scripture declares. You can certainly pick and choose whatever scriptures suit your cause, just as the writer of the piece at the beginning of the chapter has done, but that doesn't negate the reality that homosexuality is a sin and sin cannot abide in God's presence (Habakkuk 1:13a).

My question is: when is sin no longer sin? If one can receive forgiveness for a sin it doesn't mean it would be all right for them to continue in that sin. If they could, then why would Christ have had to die at all?

Paul's letter to the gentile believers in Rome reveals that some people had turned themselves against God by the depraved immorality they had become involved in. Homosexuality is listed clearly as a shameful act (Romans 1:27). Having sexual relations with the same sex is not at all what God intended. No matter whether someone is decadent in their lifestyle, shunning God altogether or attends church each time the doors are open and does wonderful things for others throughout their life, a sin still remains a sin. If our good works could get us into heaven, then again I ask, why did Jesus have to die? Now ultimately, it's God's call. God decides, not me or any other mortal man; however, those who feel they are safe under the umbrella of God's grace while freely practice immoral behavior which is termed as impure and shameful in God's Word are playing with fire. And as we all know, if you play with fire you get burnt.

Those who do as they please believing that they should be able to live their lives as they so choose are right…they can. Having said that, might I refer to Proverbs 14:12 which states: *"There is a way that appears to be right, but in the end it leads to death."* Those who have lived sinful lives, accepting only the parts of the gospel message they agree with, will likely stand in stunned silence on Judgment Day.

None of us live perfect lives. The difference is that a genuine believer in Christ has a desire to emulate their Lord, not fashion their own lives with God infused into it. That would be like buying a nutritional drink that had 5% real fruit juice infused into it. I want all God has for me, not just the things that make me feel warm and fuzzy. It concerns me that gay Christians may be flirting with danger by sidestepping the reality of their sin.

God Made Me This Way

There are some homosexuals who declare that God made them gay and loves them the way they are. I am not aware of any scripture that says or even insinuates that. God would have to contradict Himself for that to be true. Since there is no falseness in Him contradiction is impossible. That would be like saying God created Adolf Hitler to be a dictator or Charles Manson to be a mass murderer. That's just plain ridiculous. God places in each of us a sense of right and wrong and then gives us a free will to choose what we will do with the life He's given us. Our thoughts, influences, things we are taught, associations and so on help make us who we are as individuals. He didn't make some people gay and others straight. That's simply a way of justifying what one believes to be true and right.

The thought that God made homosexuals the way they are resembles Calvinism in a way. Calvinism, named after the theologian John Calvin (1509-1564) speaks of pre-destination. God made some to go to heaven and others to go to hell and there is nothing they can do to alter their path. Calvin claims that our eternal destination has been pre-determined for us from birth, thus negating 'free will'. I don't happen to agree with predestination and I don't believe homosexuals are created that way either. It's not like a person who is born with some sort of physical condition or disease. We are talking about the way people live their lives.

Hate is Not an Option

We see so much hate in the world today. In the name of Christ some churches lead protests that fly in the face of all God stands for. They spew hate and misinterpret scripture to get their point across. This does nothing but drive people away from God. Not knowing any better, non-believers lump all Christians together and view us all as feeling the same way as these hate mongers, who's insensitive and unnecessary statements throw salt on already gaping wounds.

A well-publicized elementary school shooting is a case in point. A church that has become well known for their protests of soldiers' funerals was planning to protest the funeral of those slain up in the small Connecticut community. It was reported that their main theme for the event was that God sent the shooter to punish all the sinners in that community. Pardon my language, but that has to be one of the most asinine, insensitive statements I've ever heard and that type of thing is one reason why people turn and run from Christians.

I've seen pictures of so-called Christians carrying placards at rallies that read "GOD HATES GAYS!" That's a lie!! If you ever wondered why there is so much tension between Christians and the homosexual community you have to look no further than incidents such as that. God does *not* hate homosexuals. He despises their lifestyle, but not them as individuals.

It's my opinion that people hate what they don't understand. Gays are not to be hated at all. Those who do so are wrong and unless they repent and change their ways God will take care of their intolerance and ignorance at the proper time. We are to show all people the same mercy and grace God has shown us.

I cannot begin to relate to the homosexual way of life and I will never understand why they have this penchant for coming out of the closet and announcing to the world they are gay, but that becomes irrelevant in the light of eternity. It's my sincere hope that they come to the understanding that it's their *lifestyle* that is highly displeasing to God and not them as people. Just as it is never wrong to do right, it will never be right to do wrong.

As Christians, we are not to shun anyone, gays included. We also should not hate or avoid contact with anyone because they are different than us. We are to treat them like we want to be treated by others (Luke 6:31).

A Final Look

To conclude this brief look at homosexuality and the Christian, I want to repeat that sin is always going to be sin. Sin doesn't magically become all right to do just because we love God and find out that He loves us regardless of our sin. It's still sin and once Christ's blood washes it away, we are to cease from doing it. We all continue to sin after our conversion, but there is a difference between occasionally sinning and sinning as a lifestyle. Recognizing sin as sin through Holy Spirit conviction should cause us to seek forgiveness and alter our behavior. Sinning by way of a chosen lifestyle is simply ignoring the warning signs and doing as you please. God hates the sin, not the sinner. Christians who judge and condemn homosexuals or anyone else for that matter, because of their life choices are wrong in doing so and will answer for it on the last day. It is my belief that if homosexuals look at the entirety of scripture and not a handpicked grouping of verses, they will see that what I am saying is true. I pray that is the case.

───◦◦───

"After the first blush of sin comes its indifference."
Henry David Thoreau

CHAPTER 7

THE CULT OF PERSONALITY

In my readings I have found that the Cult* of Personality applied to tyrannical dictators such as Adolf Hitler, Joseph Stalin, Benito Mussolini, Francisco Franco, Ho Chi Minh and others just like them. Mass media and propaganda elevated these individuals to the *pop culture icons* of their day, to use modern day vernacular. When I think of the Cult of Personality in this day and age though, I think more of movie stars, rock stars, television personalities and athletes. It would seem that they have an unhealthy influence on their admirers thought processes. They offer their opinions on key life issues ranging everywhere from abortion to political candidates and everything in between as if we should care. In the overall scheme of things it shouldn't matter what they think; however, many young people *do* care very much. Their popularity and exposure to the public make these 'stars' instantly recognizable. Because of this the media panders to these artificially iconic individuals, giving them air time whenever possible.

The sad part in all this is that the general public buys into this whole deal, many times diving head first into their support of a given individual

---

* It should be noted that I are not referring to a cult by its traditional definition; the usage of such a word is meant to show that those I have listed as members of the Cult of Personality have loyal followers, not unlike a traditional religious cult (which I touch on later in the this chapter), but very much different in that their followers are not required to follow, they do so of their own volition. - rlk

for reasons that run the gamut. They listen to anything and everything these people have to say and attempt to model their lives after them with the style of clothes they wear, as well as their hairstyles. Many would balk at the term 'sheep', but honestly, following after others who have what we think we want doesn't make *them* iconic, it makes us followers, like sheep.

This 'obsession' with the latest trend can become dangerous when it takes the place of God in our lives. No one but God can save our soul. Having fun is fine, but when we worship the creature rather than the creator it becomes a bit of a problem. It's all in the devil's plan to lure people away from God.

The question for Christians becomes how to deal with such a rampant situation. We are already viewed in many sectors as 'kill-joys'. People don't want to hear what we have to say perhaps because we say it in a way that doesn't show the mercy and grace of God, but rather reeks of judgment instead. When Jesus came to dine with Zacchaeus (Luke 19:1-10) He was criticized for dining with a sinner. He didn't come into the house and judge Zacchaeus for his lifestyle. The Spirit of God was upon Jesus and Zacchaeus was compelled to change his ways. Perhaps we are not tapping into the Spirit the way we are meant to. Although we will never be perfect as Christ was, this should never stop us from striving to be more and more like Him each day. I fail in my efforts to be like Christ every day, but I am stilled loved by God and His Spirit still resides within me. Tomorrow is another day and another opportunity to show the grace and mercy of God to someone.

Ungodly Behavior

There is a groundswell of support in the world today for ungodly behavior to be accepted as normal. Everything from the legalization of abortions to the absolute rejection of Christianity as an acceptable belief system is in play with protests for and against dotting the landscape. People simply don't want to be told what they can and cannot do. No two people can exist without some compromise. Consideration for another person's thoughts, opinions and feelings must exist. Without it there is friction. Enough friction will cause a fire. A fire will turn into a blaze. A blaze can rage out of control, destroying everything in its path.

Generally speaking, people don't want to be forced to adhere to rules of decency. They would rather make up their own. There are millions of decent, moral people around the globe; however, there are those who accept the idea that we shouldn't be stopped from doing as we choose regarding ethical or moral issues. Many would like to see certain laws loosened up or eliminated altogether. Some people believe they should be able to do whatever they want as long as it doesn't negatively impact anyone. This ends up being irrational, because in the end someone somewhere is always negatively impacted in one way or another.

When it comes to the Cult of Personality itself, their own true identity begins to become lost within the bright light of their own popularity. Initially, they bask in the glow of their own intense light, ignited by publicity hounds that are looking for the next big story. Always in the spotlight, they begin to crave it. When their light begins to fade, they may say or do outlandish things in an attempt to reignite their light. Their values are undermined by their own actions as they attempt to stay in vogue. These folks are human just like we are. They bleed just like us and are in need of forgiveness and mercy like anyone else. They are built up to iconic status only to be gently nudged off the cliff by the next new 'Cult' member. They need prayer, just as we all do. We need to see them as God sees them; they are all precious in His sight.

There are even those who are unwilling 'Cult' members; talent laden believers who have been built up by religious leaders and the social media just to create a buzz. No matter how distasteful it may be to them, they get caught up in the swirl of the 'Personality' whirlpool just the same and sometimes leave the "Christian scene" as a result. The whole concept of 'Christ first, me last' gets lost in a flurry of strings and a crescendo. Lost in all of this is the message. The good news of Christ gets drown out by the noise that is meant to proclaim it. The righteous ones in the body then see fit to shoot our own wounded rather than tend to their wounds and restore them back to spiritual health.

Our Mission

"He must become greater, I must become lesser." (John 3:30)

In a world where a person's status and stature mean so much we read the words of John the Baptist. He must become less important than Christ, for he was a precursor to the Messiah and not the Messiah himself. He pointed the way to the Messiah. He was to now step aside and allow Christ to come into the forefront. It would be Christ who would complete what God sent Him to accomplish, not John. It was Christ who would bear the guilt, shame and separation that was due *us*. It was Christ who would be murdered and buried, only a fond memory to His followers. And it was Christ who did what He said He would when He rose from the dead to new life. Therefore John had to become lesser; for he was not the one who would or could do all that Christ was destined in God's providence to do. No other religious leader proclaimed to be the Son of God and no other accomplished all that Christ did. Christ stands alone, as He should; the one who by His own death paid the debt that mankind owed yet could never pay.

How do we as believers deal with the 'Cult of Personality'? We need to pray for these folks. We need to ask God in all His mercy to enter into their spheres of influence and begin to chip away at the stony heart that has resisted God all these years. Maybe they knew God at one point and slid away from His warm embrace. It's not too late until God says it's too late.

The Southwest Radio Church opens each radio broadcast with the following words: "God is still on the throne and prayer changes things." God has not taken a vacation; He hasn't abdicated His throne. He still sits there, surveying all that He has created. He is such that one single, solitary word can completely change everything in a person's situation. *Prayer activates change.* When we speak to God He hears us and we can count on the fact that He has set in motion the proper answer to our request. No one can stop His will from being manifest. No one can thwart His plans. So when I say that we need to pray for the non-believers of this world, I truly believe that God is at work as we speak making this happen for the greater good and His greatest glory. God allows many things that may not benefit us in the 'right now', but it is in the 'not yet' where we will see His answer bloom and grow.

It's our responsibility to not become enraptured by the 'Cult of Personality', but rather to keep all things in perspective and seek the face of God on their behalf. They may not know their soul's condition, but we do and we know who can help them. Just imagine what they might do if they were energized by God's Holy Spirit. Now God doesn't need a big name celebrity as His personal mouthpiece, however, a celebrity with the proper humility and humble spirit; one who realizes his place in God's order of things, can be a mighty blessing to a whole lot of people.

Traditional Cults

Cult - a system of religious veneration and devotion directed toward a particular figure or object; a relatively small group of people having religious beliefs or practices regarded by others as strange or sinister; a misplaced or excessive admiration for a particular person or thing.

Let's take a brief look at cults in the traditional sense; those that are considered 'false religions'. There are two main things cults do that make them unbiblical in the eyes of the Christian and God. To know these two things is to expose them for what they truly are. 1) A true cult will alter the Bible to fit their teachings; and 2) they will present an alternate 'truth' which is typically devoid of any mention of Christ, His redemptive work on the cross or His blood being the only way to receive forgiveness for sin.

Since this is not a book on cults, I am not going to take the time to break down each and every religious group that is listed by the mainline churches to be considered cultic in nature and beliefs. Instead, I wanted to touch briefly on the whole concept of cults and how they cheapen the reality of true redemption.

On the whole, any teaching that lessens Christ's role in the entirety of the redemptive process is cultic. Any teaching that disavows the Bible as God's inerrant word and His *only* word to His people is cultic. Any teaching that denies the Trinity or tries to add to the Word of God is cultic. Other religions and cults preach about happiness, peace, satisfaction and even discipline; however, none of them speak of Christ coming to pay for the sin of all mankind, thus saving them from the wrath of God.

I will touch on some of the other global religions like Buddhism, Hinduism and Islam in the next chapter, but suffice it to say that the reality of God coming to earth in human form to give men a living example of who He is and what He was willing to do to bridge the gap sin had created between God and man is unparalleled throughout history.

No other religion can say that; nor can any cult. Mankind in their effort to improve themselves on their *own* terms has invented various religious entities that end up being in direct conflict with the Bible. The leader(s) get caught up in the power associated with leading others and end up being the focus of their own mini-Cult of Personality. It isn't national in scope, but rather confined to the local participants. The focal point becomes the leader rather than God and though the Bible may be read, its meaning is often times skewed towards a point the self-appointed leader is trying to make. It's a dangerous situation when man trifles with the things of God.

We saw that with Vernon Howell, aka, David Koresh in Waco, TX back in the early 1990's. After being excommunicated from the Seventh Day Adventist Church due to a disagreement on scriptural interpretation, Howell was invited by a friend to attend a group called The Branch Davidians. Over time, Vernon Howell legally changed his name to David Koresh, and assumed the leadership of the group. Koresh fancied himself as the "final prophet" from God. The U.S. Bureau of Alcohol, Tobacco, Firearms & Explosives raided the cult's compound and the resulting siege ended with the compound burning to the ground. The bodies of Koresh, 54 adults & 28 children were found dead after the fire was extinguished.[9]

We also saw that with Jim Jones and the Peoples Temple. Jones began preaching back in the 1950's and in the mid-1960's moved his religious group to Northern California. By the early 1970's he started the People's Temple in San Francisco. Feeling paranoid and disturbed by public perception, Jones purchased land in Guyana and ended up moving his then 1,000 member church there. The small village he had built was named Jonestown. Rather than a paradise, it was run like a prison camp with sparse food given out and armed guards at the grounds parameter. Fearful of a plot against him, Jones had numerous suicide drills to test the member's loyalty. He finally did force his followers to participate in a mass 'revolutionary' suicide against the inhumanity in the world by drinking cyanide-laced grape Flavor-Aid, with a sedative added. All 914 members died on the grounds of their Jonestown, Guyana compound in November of 1978. Jones was found dead from mortal gunshot wound to the head. [10]

The common theme in these and many other cultic examples is power and control, the result of which is a type of 'Cult of Personality' where the leader was viewed as larger than life and far more important and powerful then he actually was. This is the danger that results from people seeking peace, love, hope and contentment outside of God Himself. They find themselves drawn to individuals who are charismatic and become subject to the lies of these masterful manipulators of half-truths and fiction. Once in these gatherings of enlightenment they find that they must either follow along with all that is taught and commanded or be punished; in some cases perhaps even die. Now these are extreme examples. The common religious groups generally associated with the term 'cult' are not like that at all. They are, however, in direct contradiction of Biblical teaching and that's a major problem.

This is why it is imperative for individuals to seek the face of God and ask for wisdom and discernment regarding the things of God. Don't solely rely on the words of others, but use that to supplement your own Biblical investigation. Hitch your spiritual wagon to those you know in your heart you can trust. Once you begin to know scripture, you can better determine who is of God and who is not. This is largely what the Holy Spirit is for, to lead and guide us into all wisdom and knowledge. If not careful, we can easily be carted off into a direction we never intended to go.

A Quick Look at Scientology

Scientology was developed back in the 1952 by science fiction and fantasy author, L. Ron Hubbard. A 'religion' created by a science fiction / fantasy author. Let that sink in for a minute. It's really nothing more than another way for man to circumvent God. Let's simply sidestep the whole issue by making up something new and different. While we're at it let's make it a money making proposition by charging people to become a part of our newly invented way to enlightenment and power.

I can sum up this 'cult' with one quote from Hubbard himself: "*The way to make a million dollars is to start a religion.*" [11] I think that pretty much sums up his heart's motivation, don't you think?

It's nothing more than an invented religion where you eventually (if you pay enough) become your own god. Each level you must achieve has a price tag associated with it. I don't believe it's anything to be even remotely considered valid since in reality it's a business and not a religion at all.

A Different Kind of Church

In the fall of 2011 I had returned to New Jersey from Texas, where I had previously lived the last nine years. I was looking for a good church to attend and in the course of striking up a conversation with the teller at my new bank, found myself invited to their church. I was excited at the prospect and attended there for several weeks.

Now I'm not perfect by any stretch of the imagination and I don't know everything there is to know about the Bible either, but I know more than the average person and I also sought the discernment the Holy Spirit that is available to any believer for the asking. Something didn't seem right. One clue was that the preacher spoke for well over an hour, yet I found that he was constantly repeating himself, which I found unnecessary. Then he said something comical and upon getting a laugh repeated that same comical line six more times over the course of the message. The speaker made his point and then pounded it home over and over and over again. I got up before he was finished and never returned. An assistant minister whom I had become friendly with called me up and said he noticed I left early, was there a problem? I told him a little bit to which he responded, *"I told you we were a different kind of church."*

I decided later to write him an email. Now it's no secret that I can be a little blunt at times. It comes from being raised in Jersey I guess. I laid out my problems with what I saw and heard going on there and in the course of my email criticized the pastor for several things. Perhaps I was wrong for doing that, but I didn't like what I was hearing. It had become very clear to me that this church felt they had tapped into the 'real' truth of the bible and not just what everyone else was preaching and teaching.

The woman from the bank who had been so friendly to me the first time I came in literally turned her back on me the next time I went in. Apparently the person I had written to told others about my email. I never heard from that assistant minister again. 'Don't agree with me and I will shun you' is not how we win people to Christ or welcome Christian visitors into our churches. Maybe I have it all wrong. But I shook the dust from my feet and moved on. I now attend a very much alive and loving Presbyterian Church whose Pastor is 'born again' and exudes the love, mercy and grace of God.

We need to be very careful where we partake of our spiritual food. Just because we're told they are good Christians or that there is sound teaching at this or that church doesn't mean they are or it is. We need to make sure to use our spiritual radar. Those who truly seek God will find the right church for them. Places where you feel welcome; a place of worship where you get blessed and where you are able to be a blessing. I make it a practice to ask the Lord to reveal to me very clearly where He would like me to attend. God alone knows the heart of the pastor and the congregation. There is no doubt in my mind that if we let Him, God will lead us to a church that is just right for us.

———————

"God cannot give us a happiness and peace apart from Himself, because it is not there. There is no such thing."

C. S. Lewis

CHAPTER 8

Buddhism, Hinduism & Islam

The purpose of this chapter is to inform believers, whether new or experienced, regarding the basics of the three main religions that exist besides the Judeo-Christian belief system. I will provide their main beliefs, how they compare to Christianity and how we view each other. While there are many beliefs other than these three, some of which I briefly touch on elsewhere in the book, I would consider these to be the most globally prominent.

Buddhism

"Buddhism began in India about 500 years before the birth of Christ. Buddhism, unlike Hinduism, can point to a specific founder. However, in Buddhism, like so many other religions, fanciful stories arose concerning events in the life of the founder, Siddhartha Gautama (fifth century BC). Buddha wrote nothing, and the writings that have come down to us date from about 150 years after his death.

Deep in meditation, Siddhartha Gautama reached the highest degree of God- consciousness, known as nirvana. He supposedly stayed under the fig tree for seven days. After that, the fig tree was called the bodhi, or the bo tree, the tree of wisdom. The truths he learned he would now impart to the world, no longer as Siddhartha Gautama, but as the Buddha, the Enlightened One. The Indian people, disillusioned with Hinduism, listened intently to Buddha's teaching. By the time of Buddha's death, at the age of 80, his teachings had become a strong force in India. Buddha made a diagnosis of suffering, to which Buddhists give the name of the Four Noble Truths."

The Four Noble Truths

1. "Everything in life is subject to suffering and frustration.
2. The cause of this suffering and disease is desire – craving, lust, attachment to people and things, even to life itself.
3. To escape from suffering, men must crush all desire and craving, and break all the chains of attachment.
4. The way to do this is by following the Noble Eight-fold Path. This alone can lead to nirvana, the ultimate goal of all Buddhist teaching.

The Noble Eight-fold Path

1. Right belief: recognition and understanding of the Four Noble Truths.
2. Right intention: the disciple sets himself to the single-minded pursuit of the goal and makes this his aim.
3. Right speech: watching one's words and seeking to avoid deceptive and uncharitable speech, idle chatter and gossip.
4. Right action: avoidance of wrongdoing; behavior to be motivated by selflessness and charity.
5. Right livelihood: not following an occupation which would cause harm to other beings.
6. Right effort: patient striving to prevent and eliminate evil impulses and to foster and develop good ones.
7. Right mindfulness: seeking self-awareness through steady attention to thoughts, feelings and actions.

8. *Right concentration: combines with right effort and right mindfulness in the spiritual discipline which enables the disciple to overcome all that holds him back in his search for nirvana.*

The 5 Buddhist Precepts

1. *Kill no living thing (including insects)*
2. *Do not steal*
3. *Do not commit adultery*
4. *Tell no lies*
5. *Do not drink intoxicants or take drugs"[12]*

The Buddhism – Christianity Comparison

The essence of Buddhism is to cease from all desire, to attain virtue and to purify the heart. There are significant differences between Christianity and Buddhism. Christians believe in one creator God; Buddhists deny the existence of a personal creator and Lord. They claim that the world operates by natural power and law rather than divine command. Christians not only believe in one personal God, but also believe that He is the only one that is to be worshipped. Buddhists deified Buddha, who was a mortal that reached a self-appointed enlightened stage of deep mediation. They also worship other gods. Christians believe that although sin affects all it touches, it is ultimately against God. Because of that, a savior for man is needed. Buddhists believe no such thing. Christians believe that man is of infinite worth, made in the image of God. Buddhism teaches that man is totally worthless and living in a temporary existence. The main doctrines of Christianity are constant without change and accepted by all true Bible believing

Christians. Buddhism has many sects and their beliefs take on many forms. There is no consistency.

Since they deny the existence of the Judeo-Christian God, they could be considered by some to be a cult. Their teachings are somewhat inspiring and have some validity due to the nature of them, but teaching that a mere mortal is like a god and that all desire is essentially sin is in direct contradiction with God's Word. Naturally, disbelieving in the existence of God and as a result His Word eliminates the contradiction and allows for any and all other human thought to be seen as far more important than it ever would be otherwise. The creature is once again stepping over the creator in the attempt to replace Him.

Hinduism

"**Hinduism** is practiced primarily in India, Bangladesh, Sri Lanka, and Nepal. It is a diverse family of devotional and ascetic cults and philosophical schools, all sharing a belief in reincarnation and involving the worship of one or more of a large pantheon of gods and goddesses…. Hindu society was traditionally based on a caste system.

Karma and Rebirth - the nature of one's actions—and the attitude with which actions were performed—was believed to have determinative consequences over one's future, both in this lifetime and in future rebirths. … good karma obviously would entail a better rebirth, bad karma results in a worse existence.

Dharma – doing one's dharma means not only remaining ethical but also assuming the duties that are proper to the

class or caste one is born into (due to one's past karma),
and to the stage of life one is presently in. Inequalities in the
present life are regarded as a result of differing past karma,
and the inequalities of a projected future will reflect the
rewards and punishments of actions done in the present:
"Now people here whose behavior is pleasant can expect
to enter a pleasant womb, like that of a woman of the
Brahman [the priestly class], the Ksatriya [the warrior
class], of the Vaisya [agriculturalist and trader] class. But
people of foul behavior can expect to enter a foul womb, like
that of a dog, a pig, or an outcaste woman" (Chandogya
Upanishad, 5.10.7)."[13]

The Hindu - Christianity Comparison

Hinduism is very much different than Christianity. It claims to
be the oldest religion, yet doesn't have a founder or a point in time
when Hinduism first began or was first practiced. The main difference
between these two belief systems is that Christianity recognizes one
omnipotent God in three persons (the Trinity), while Hinduism has at its
root thousands of gods and believes that all of them are a manifestation
of one god and one omnipotent power. Another major difference is that
Hinduism is constantly evolving, in that its rituals progress. Christianity,
on the other hand, believes Jesus Christ, the Son of God, to be the central
and vitally essential part of Christianity.

We find a significant difference in the attitudes of these religions and
their followers in that Hindu's tolerate Christianity, while Christians are
totally, yet not actively, opposed to Hinduism. Christians believe that any
other form of worship that is not approved by the Bible is an anathema or
accursed and a sin against Almighty God. The Hindu people essentially

believe that 'All roads lead to the top of the mountain', while Christians believe that Jesus Christ is the only way to get to Heaven. Christianity teaches that there's no salvation outside of the blood sacrifice made by Jesus Christ. Christians believe that there will come on a final day known only by God when there will be a judgment of all deeds. Believers in Christ will stand before *Him* on that day before what is called the Bema Seat of Christ. Their eternal destination will not be determined on that day, for God's Holy Spirit has sealed their redemption on the day of their conversion. What they have done on behalf of Christ with the gifts they have been given shall be judged with the result being rewards in heaven. Unbelievers shall stand before God Almighty at the White Throne Judgment. Here both the living and the dead who have rejected Christ and whose names are not found in the *"lambs book of life"* (Rev 21:27) shall be cast into a lake of fire for all eternity. Hindus believe that each person is judged and punished by his own karma. They believe in the reincarnation or rebirth of the soul or spirit, after physical death. It's at that time that they begin a new life in a new body that may be human, animal or spiritual depending on the moral quality of the previous life's actions. A distinct belief of Hindus is that they believe everything possesses a part of God; therefore God exists in both good and evil. Christians believe God is ubiquitous, in that He is present, appearing, or found everywhere, yet they do not believe that God is *in* everything, such as a rock, piece of furniture or tree; nor do they believe that He created evil. Christianity teaches that God created mankind with the freedom to choose. Within that free will is the possibility of doing wrong.

In one of my readings on Hinduism there was a section at the bottom for comments. One Hindu seriously made the comment that it was ridiculous to believe in Christianity because it was too confusing. He went on to say that Hinduism was *"a lot less confusing, fulfilling and more fun."* I'd like to believe that this was a child who wrote that, but I have no way of knowing the writer's age. From the lack of depth in his comment, I find it scary that someone would honestly choose one 'religion' over another because it was "more fun". The remainder of his comment showed a severe ignorance towards the Christian system of belief.

In Hinduism, there is no mention of sin, per se, although evil does exist. Hinduism deals with evil and sin on an individual basis through karma or in effect, an apparent delay in their rise to enlightenment. Like Buddhism, Christians would consider Hinduism a cult due to the nature of their belief system. The focus is on themselves and on many gods. They strive to live the best life they are able to on their own without any divine assistance. In Christianity, man's sin is the reason Christ needed to come to earth. A blood sacrifice needed to be made to hold back the wrath of God. [14]

Islam

*"**Islam** – the religion of the Muslims, a monotheistic faith regarded as revealed through Muhammad as the Prophet of Allah (God). Founded in the Arabian Peninsula in the 7th century AD, Islam is now the professed faith of more than a billion people worldwide, particularly in North Africa, the Middle East, and parts of Asia. The ritual observances and moral code of Islam were said to have been given to Muhammad as a series of revelations, which were codified in the Qu'ran. Islam is regarded by its adherents as the last of the revealed religions, and Muhammad is seen as the last of the prophets, building on and perfecting the examples and teachings of Abraham, Moses, and Jesus. There are two major branches in Islam: Sunni and Shia."* [15]

The 11 ways Islam is similar to Christianity:

- *There is only one God. He is the Creator and Sustainer of the universe.*
- *God sent prophets such as Abraham, Moses, David, Joseph, John the Baptist, Jesus, etc.*
- *People should follow the Ten Commandments and the moral teachings of the prophets.*
- *Mary, the mother of Jesus, was a virgin; therefore Jesus was born miraculously.*
- *Jesus Christ is the Messiah and he performed miracles.*
- *The Old testament/Torah and the new testament/Gospel) are Holy Scriptures.*
- *Satan is evil; therefore, people should not follow Satan.*
- *An Anti-Christ will appear on Earth before the Day of Judgment.*
- *Jesus Christ will return by descending from Heaven and will kill the Anti-Christ.*
- *The Day of Judgment will occur and people will be judged.*
- *There is hell and paradise.*

The 3 main differences between Islam and Christianity:

1. *Christians believe in the Trinity, meaning that God has 3 forms (Father, Son, Holy Spirit). While in the religion of Islam the Trinity is totally rejected. Jesus is neither God, nor the Son of God. They believe Jesus was a human prophet and not divine.*
2. *The Qu'ran says Jesus did not die on the cross, but God made it appear that way to people. Furthermore, the Qu'ran also says that Jesus was ascended to Heaven by God. Most Christians today insist*

Jesus was crucified and died on the cross, but two days later was resurrected just as He said He would.

3. Christians believe in the concept of "Original Sin" which means that human beings are born as sinners, bearing the burden of the "Original Sin" of Adam and Eve. Muslims do not believe in the 'Original Sin' for two main reasons: In the Qu'ran, God forgave Adam for what he has done and according to the Qu'ran, no one should be made to bear the burden of someone else's sin or mistake because it is unfair.

The Islamic view of Christianity

1. The true teachings of Jesus are fully compatible with Islam. Muslims are the true followers of the teachings of Jesus, Moses, and Mohammad.

2. Muslims regard the "real" Bible (that reflects God's actual message and the real teachings of Jesus and the prophets before him) as a holy scripture. (They) believe current Bible is corrupted, but not completely false. So, (they) can still find today in the Bible some traces of the truth, such as verses that contradict with the Trinity. That is why Muslims are willing to accept the "current" Bible only to the extent that it does not contradict with the Qu'ran.

3. Modern Christianity was not founded by Jesus, but rather by Paul and the Romans in the Council of Nicaea in 325 AD (meaning about 325 years after Jesus), inspired by Satan. In the Council of Nicaea, church leaders from around the world debated and finally decided on what should and shouldn't be included in the Bible. For Christianity to be adopted by the Roman Empire as its official religion, it had to succumb to the desires of the Romans who wanted to incorporate their own pagan religious beliefs and myths into Christianity. The

integrity of the message brought by Jesus from God was compromised to appease the Roman Empire. Christianity has evolved into a cult that has deviated significantly from the true teachings of Jesus by: (a) adding new doctrines not preached by Jesus, (b) deleting or modifying some of the teachings of Jesus, and (c) creating an "unholy", man-made scripture. A holy scripture must be in the form and content intended, inspired, or revealed by God, not created by human beings.

4. *Many Christians insist that Muslims do not worship the same God of Christianity. (Muslims) say that Islam requires (them) to worship only God (the God of Abraham, Moses, Jesus and Mohammad), the creator of the universe. The Qu'ran instructs (Muslims) to worship only the creator of the universe and not worship any human being. (According to the teachings of Islam) Muslims today are the true followers of the teachings of Jesus Christ, as well as the teachings of Prophet Mohammad and the other prophets before them. Muslims worship the God of Jesus, the God who created Jesus and whom Jesus himself worshipped."*[16]

In answer to the question "How do Muslims feel about Christians?" I received one intriguing response: *"We atheists would actually side with the Christians on this one. Christians are aiming for world superiority. Muslims are aiming for world domination and put their religion into Law…. Which one scares you more?"*

For the sake of clarification, this atheist has it wrong; Christians do not seek world superiority. It's my sincere hope that he didn't come up with this notion from Christians in his circle of influence for if that is true, the problem may be worse than I had first thought. We seek to introduce the world to a benevolent deity who will forgive them of every sin, reveal to them a better way to live and in so doing have the world find true and lasting peace which leads to fulfillment and hope.

The Final Analysis

Scripture states clearly that Jesus was the Son of God (Luke 1:35; John 5:18; John 3:16; 1 John 5:20), yet all three of these religions have seen fit to ignore that fact. They either view him as a good teacher or moral man or they don't mention him at all. The Muslims contention that God made it look like Jesus died on the cross and rose again to new life, when in actually God ascended Christ into heaven is confusing; this because while they say they believe that Jesus was the Messiah, they also say that he was just a prophet, there was nothing special or divine about him. It is unclear why Jesus would be taken up to heaven and not Moses or Mohammed, the two other prophets they make mention of. It is also unclear why a human prophet would be the one they believe would return to defeat the anti-Christ.

The fact that Muslims believe that modern Christianity as it is preached and taught today is satanic in origin is interesting in that it appears to be based on conjecture and not on any actual facts. That belief would of course negate all scripture that doesn't agree with their own version of scripture set down by the prophet Mohammed. Their disqualification of modern scripture of course paves the way for acceptance of the Qu'ran, which they have deemed the perfect word of God. Am I the only one who finds that rather convenient?

The Bible is clear regarding anyone who disputes or alters one word that has been written in scripture.

> "I warn everyone who hears the words of the prophecy of
> this scroll: If any one of you adds anything to them, God will
> add to you the plagues described in this scroll. And if any
> one of you takes words away from this scroll of prophecy,
> God will take away from you your share in the tree of life

and in the Holy City, which are described in this scroll."
(Revelation 22:18-19)

Buddhists and Hindus appear more passive, with their beliefs based more on morality, ethics and personal enlightenment. Islam comes across as more restrictive and demanding.

It seems odd to me that Hinduism would just rise up seemingly out of nowhere to become such a large religion. It may be the oldest, but is appears to also be the most simplistic. Buddhists, apparently feel the same way regarding Christians as Hindus in that they seem more intent on reaching their nirvana state of well being and happiness than squabbling with those who believe something far different.

Muslims look to take a more aggressive approach to this whole belief issue. Their beliefs disallow coexistence with modern Christianity for the mere fact that Satan, according to them, was instrumental in influencing the scriptures at the council of Nicaea. Essentially, that validates the Qu'ran, which is accepted as divine writings dictated to the prophet Mohammed by the archangel Gabriel. If it doesn't agree with the Qu'ran, then the Bible is seen to be wrong and not the Quran due to alleged Satanic involvement. Where they get this notion is unsubstantiated to the best of my knowledge since no one alive today was alive to report on the Counsel at Nicaea.

The Bible stands on its own and while certain translations may differ slightly in the phraseology used, the same intent and message is brought forth. The Bible is either wholly God's word or it isn't. The writing of the Qu'ran violates the scripture previously cited earlier in this chapter.

Christianity is monotheistic in that it believes in one God and one God only. Polytheistic religions are ones who have more than one god. They believe there cannot be one god with all the power and authority; it must be dispersed among the other gods. Therefore we have a god of the sea, a god of the air, a god of the weather, etc. Henotheism believes there are many gods and yet followers serve only one of the many. The problem with this is that the one God of the Jewish and Christian faith declares that He is the one God that is to be worshipped.[17] All others are false and followers of them shall be cast into the lake of fire on the final day. If the Bible is accurate, those who refuse to believe in the one true God choosing rather to follow a more palatable route to heaven will be shocked when the final day arrives and time is no more.

Summing Things Up

So if I were to sum up each religion with a single statement I would say the following:

1. Buddhism – purging all cravings and desire ultimately leads to their singular goal … nirvana, a state of perfect happiness.
2. Hinduism – the nature of one's attitude and actions determines their future rebirth; good is repaid with good, bad with bad.
3. Islam – one God, no savior; they follow the Qu'ran rather than the Bible, claiming the Bible is corrupted through false interpretation and translation.

I trust that this has been helpful. I tried to break it down into simple, bite size pieces for I don't believe the average believer needs to know all the finer points of these religions unless they so desire to take the plunge into such a scholarly endeavor.

"I feel sorry for Christians, because most of them are good people and they believe in a religion corrupted by evil priests who were influenced by Satan himself."

"The Qur'an is very clear about this. Islam is the only way and all non-believers are infidel and must be converted, or destroyed, or in some cases taxed."

Two different Muslims answering my question:
'How do Muslims feel about Christians?'

"This is how you can recognize the Spirit of God: Every spirit that acknowledges that Jesus Christ has come in the flesh is from God, but every spirit that does not acknowledge Jesus is not from God. This is the spirit of the antichrist, which you have heard is coming and even now is already in the world."
1 John 4:2-3

CHAPTER 9

WHAT ABOUT SIN?

It's very interesting to me that those who have decided not to believe in God sidestep the whole question of sin or disobedience to Him. People in general don't seem to have much of a problem acknowledging the fact that they aren't perfect, but the whole question of 'sin' seems to be a stumbling block for them. It's very normal for people to think: 'what did I do that was so terrible? I didn't kill anyone or sell drugs to little kids or anything like that.' The problem with that line of thinking is that it raises the question of standards or more specifically, what standards need to be followed. As I mentioned in Chapter 2, there *has* to be some standard to go by. Whose rules should we follow? Will the rules I set for myself be suitable for my neighbor or the people in the next town? Would they be acceptable across state lines? How about across borders into other countries? You see, it's a lot more than just setting up and following a list of rules. There has to be a sense of fairness to them. Each person can't establish his or her own set of standards to follow. They have to be universally accepted by the majority of those affected by them. Who decides what's fair and just and what isn't? Our local, state and federal governments are supposed to be doing that, yet all the rules and laws in the world won't help us behave better; for as the saying goes: 'You can't legislate morality.' You can't make people live a certain lifestyle ethically or morally, nor should law force them to. People should be able to choose how they will live ethically and morally;

that is exactly what Christianity affords people - the free-will to choose how they will live.

We truly *can* live anyway we choose; however, there are consequences that go with each decision we make. Take God; whether you believe in Him or not doesn't change reality … it doesn't change a thing except how you live your own life and the way you look at things. Let's say you have determined that you don't believe in God. What about sin? Without a God to sin against, you don't even have to deal with that question.

For the sake of argument let's assume for the moment that there *is* a God and that sin *does* exist. What exactly *is* sin? According to the Oxford Dictionary sin is the following: "*a transgression of a religious or moral law, especially when deliberate; deliberate disobedience to the known will of God; a condition of estrangement from God resulting from such disobedience; something regarded as being shameful, deplorable, or utterly wrong.*"[18]

It just so happens that the above definition lines up with the definition a Bible believing Jew or Christian would believe. Jews see sin as: "*a passing over or rejection of the will of God. The primary cause of sin is the evil inclination.*"[19] Christians believe essentially the same thing: disobedience to God that started in the Garden of Eden with Adam and Eve.

The Big 3 and Sin

Believers of Islam see sin somewhat differently. There are ninety different words in the Qur'an for sin. Suffice it to say that Mohammed's mission was "*addressed to humans who are in grave danger because of their propensity to sin.*"[20] Muslims believe "*there are many ways in which humans fall into sin or error, and the Qur'an offers guidance so that there can be no doubt what behavior God requires. The Day of Judgment is decided on an exact balance between good and evil acts—though evaluation takes account of intention. But God is merciful and compassionate, and the way of repentance is always open."*[21] Just how this repentance is dispensed isn't disclosed. It should be assumed that God arbitrarily gives it.

Hindus believe *"the most radical fault which has to be overcome is not so much sin as ignorance. Nevertheless, it is perfectly well recognized that there are behaviors (and thoughts) which are wrong and which might well be called sin."*[22] They have greater and lesser offenses. The way to deal with offenses is to undertake penance and make atonement. Their penance seems to range from meditation or the use of fire to somehow burn out the offense to giving gifts to religious leaders or making pilgrimages.

Since Buddhists don't accept the belief that there is one omnipotent deity, then the whole system within that belief must not exist either; at least according to them. No original sin, no need of redemption. Like the Hindus (and this appears to be the only similarity between the two), they believe in karma and have plain distinctions between good and evil deeds.

"A wrongful thought, word, or deed is one which is committed under the influence of the 'Three Roots of Evil', namely greed, hatred, and delusion. Wrongful actions are designated in various ways: as evil, bad or corrupt, and all such deeds lead inevitably to a deeper entanglement in the process of suffering and rebirth and away from the fulfillment and enlightenment of nirvana."[23]

Where's Jesus?

The serious problem that exists here is the removal of Jesus Christ from the story. He was the creator as part of the Trinity: Father, Son and Holy Spirit; however, has been stripped of His rightful place in creation. As believers in God, we have placed our trust not only in Him, but also in His word, which we believe to be the Bible; the one and only, flawless Word of God. The Muslims are the only group of the big three world religions who deal with the Jesus question. Yes, he existed. No, he was not divine. No, he did not die a gruesome death on a cross and rise from the dead three days later. Christians, who base their entire system of belief on this information, accept Christ's death as factual and therefore exactly as it is portrayed in scripture.

It appears to me that Christianity has a more cohesive story to tell. It has a beginning, middle and a predicted or prophesied end. Original sin [24] is dealt with while it is not in the other religions. The fact that evil cannot abide in the presence of God is common in Islamic beliefs as well; however, strict adherence to the Qur'an is necessary to receive salvation and even then, the decision is ultimately Gods. In Christianity, without a blood sacrifice, salvation from sin is impossible. Christ, being wholly God came to earth in the form of man to willingly die thus paying for every sin committed by all men. Christians believe Christ's death satisfied the penalty for those sins. They also believe that one drop of Christ's blood is all that is required to remove all sin from an individual seeking forgiveness.

According to Christians, a person can become as enlightened as they want to be or follow the strictest moral and ethical code known to man, but without a blood cleansing of ones sins committed in this life, they will die, be buried in the ground and be sentenced to hell for all eternity. Man wants options; he wants an easier route to heaven, so as a result, Christianity seems harsh, restrictive and intolerant. Unfortunately, life is not one big game of "Let's Make a Deal!" You can't wish away things that seem harsh or unpleasant. Certain things must be considered. Since there is no proof that God exists, maybe Christians have it all wrong. Is it possible? Sure. My question to the unbeliever is: are you willing to risk all eternity on the chance that God doesn't exist? As I quoted earlier, I agree with Albert Camus: "I would rather live my life as if there is a god and die to find out there isn't, than live my life as if there isn't and die to find out there is." The astounding thing about Albert Camus' statement is that he didn't profess to be a Christian. He was a French philosopher & writer; winner of the 1957 Nobel Peace Prize.

I find it so much simpler to embrace Christ than to delve into endless theories that cannot be proven. They are based on human wisdom, individual experience and opinion. We Christians are exercising our free will by placing our faith in God. To us it is the only sensible choice to make. Having made that choice, we find that God's presence becomes very real to us, as does the presence of His Holy Spirit in our lives. We sense a change and see things differently as a result. While non-believers may consider it nothing more than a contrived emotional response to something we feel we need in our lives, we see it quite differently. It has become alive and real to us. They want experiential. Quite frankly, a relationship with God couldn't get any more experiential. The issue is that it's all based on faith in the unseen and not on scientific facts.

Discernment

Those outside the faith largely see Christians as an arrogant, judgmental lot. Whether we intend to present ourselves that way or not, that is the perception the public has. That being said how are we to deal with this whole issue of sin when dealing with an unregenerate soul? How can we break the self-inflicted bonds we have placed ourselves in? How can we reach those who want nothing to do with God? We are in this world. We cannot escape it. As believers we are called to not live as the unbeliever. Generally speaking, unbelievers tend to have hedonistic leanings. If we stay in our churches or in our little home groups and never venture out to where they are, how will we reach them? *"On hearing this, Jesus said to them, 'It is not the healthy who need a doctor, but the sick. I have not come to call the righteous, but sinners.'"* (Mark 2:17) We don't have to become *like* them, but we can be *with* them and seek opportunities to plant seeds. We need to understand that every situation we encounter may not be right to recite the 'The Romans Road to Salvation'(*). Maybe someone just needs a friend ... someone to talk to. Maybe someone just needs a hug or a kind word. Maybe someone could use prayer. These are seeds planted in the souls of those who are lost. We need to use *discernment*, which we can receive by merely asking God. For example, spiritual discernment is when we recognize a certain situation to be one that may be conducive to planting a seed of hope, peace or the gospel itself. God knows when the time is right, as a general rule *we* absolutely do not.

Planting Seeds

I am reminded of the illustration that goes something like this: The pastor of a local church was driving home at the end of his day. He spied a homeless man huddled in a doorway not far from the church. It was a sub-freezing night. The reverend pulled his car over, grabbed a bible from a box in the back seat, got out of his car and walked up to the man. The cold air nipped at his face as he handed the shivering man the bible and said *"God bless you, brother. God loves you."* He quickly turned on his heels, got back into his warm car and drove away.

Which one of that man's needs did the pastor meet? In spite of the pastor handing the man a bible, he met *none* of that man's needs. That man didn't need a Bible right then. He needed warmth, food, drink, perhaps a place to stay. The pastor didn't know him so he didn't know his spiritual status. He could have engaged the man in conversation over

---

(*) 'The Romans Road to Salvation' is a grouping of bible verses from Paul's letter to the Romans that explains the way to forgiveness of one's sins and the subsequent entrance into God's family.

a hot cup of coffee some place warm. Maybe the man was down on his luck. Perhaps he had nowhere to go.

Maybe the man was a new Christian who was praying to God for help. Maybe the Pastor could have taken him to the local YMCA or Salvation Army. Maybe the Pastor could have done a lot of things, but he didn't. I know unsaved people who would have done a better job meeting that man's need than this fictional pastor. God gave this pastor a mission and he failed. Fortunately for him, he will have many more opportunities. God is kind, patient and loving and He needs to be because sometimes we simply just don't 'get it' … at all. What can we do to remedy this? We must learn to see others the way God sees them. The unsaved should notice a difference in us; a positive difference, not a negative one. If you are close to God and allow His Spirit to minister His mercy and grace through you then someone will be drawn to you. They will want to spend time with you. God knows how to bring people into the fold.

We are to be like an angel that drifts into and out of lives on the boardwalk during the summer, at a concert, at a party, in the mall, in the grocery store, in our own neighborhoods. Be Christ to them. We need to be extraneous, inconsequential; we are in fact quite irrelevant in the overall plan and scheme of things. They really don't even need to know who we are at times; but they definitely need to know the God we represent. We are not vital to the end result. We just need to be obedient. Plant seeds in faith or water seeds planted by others. God will bring in the harvest. *God* will.

Overzealousness

It's my belief that Christians get caught up in a 'great commission' mentality. This isn't a bad thing unless it is taken too far. In our zeal to lead others into the family of God some violate another person's 'space'. A secular example of this very thing was when I was standing in my garage one day and a man who turned out to be a salesman, marched right into my garage, reached out to shake my hand, handed me a business card and rested his hand on my work bench. He stood roughly 5 feet away from me, which was too close in my estimation. I was a little taken aback. I didn't hear much of what he said because he was violating my space big time. I eventually told him I didn't appreciate him coming into my garage without being invited and asked him to leave. Some Christians do the exact same thing when presenting the gospel to others.

Jesus never forced anyone to listen to Him and He also never took written Old Testament documents and crammed them down anyone's throat. People around Him were *compelled* to listen to Him. No one forced them to, yet they were compelled nonetheless. We can be like that too. As we mature spiritually, the Holy Spirit can flow more freely through us if we allow it to. When that happens we exude the mercy, grace and love of Christ in our countenance and demeanor. When this takes place as I said before, people will be drawn to us. This must take place for the sake of Christ and not for our own popularity. The Spirit is drawing them, not us. Those who find themselves in that position without any hidden agendas can be used of God to do great things for the kingdom.

Boldness is a great thing, but we can misuse it. We don't need to argue with unbelievers, we need to engage them in civil conversation when the door of opportunity is open. A one-on-one conversation where you demonstrate a general caring for the individual you are speaking to can be much more effective than a shouting match. We must let God lead by His Holy Spirit. He will enable us to use wisdom, discretion and discernment if we ask Him to.

Everyone's personality is different. Some are outgoing, some keep to themselves. Some are loud, some quiet. My style of evangelizing may seem soft and too casual in the face of an impending Judgment Day; however, I don't have people turning and walking away from me either. I try to give them something to think about. That is one of my reasons for writing my books; to give believers some basics based on my studies, research and experience from over 34 years of walking with the Lord. God loves the unsaved; we need to also. Judgment needs to be left up to God.

———◆———

"The safest road to hell is the gradual one - the gentle slope, soft underfoot, without sudden turnings, without milestones, without signposts."

C. S. Lewis

CHAPTER 10

RELATABILITY

Back in the fall of 2001 I was asked to leave my residence by my wife. Our marriage had been faltering for a few years and she chose this time to file for a separation. Through a cloud of uncertainty I attempted to sort out my options. A friend told me of a small Baptist Church he had attended at one time. Upon visiting, they welcomed me with open arms. The pastor introduced me to a man who was also separated from his wife and heading for divorce, just like myself. We could relate to one another. We subsequently spent a lot of time together, venting our problems, expressing our concerns and keeping each other company. Being relatable to someone is important to the healing process because it helps you realize you are not alone in your plight. There is always someone who has troubles similar or possibly identical to you.

> **to relate:** feel sympathy with; identify with; to relate to something or someone is to show or establish some sort of connection between that thing or person and yourself; to bring about a natural association.

Note: While I understand that relatability isn't a word I figured if sports announcers can make up words like 'trickeration' for *their* purposes I can make up the word 'relatability' for *mine*.

If we truly want any chance of relating to those outside the faith then I believe it must start with us staying as close to our Heavenly Father as possible. If anyone knows how to relate to others it is the creator of all things. While we strive to live godly lives, we must at least attempt to relate to those who are in the world. We aren't alone in this quest; God will assist us if we ask. As we live our lives, going with the flow of our respective days, we will be given opportunities to relate to those around us. We may not say anything but rather become relatable by our actions. At some point in our walk with God it will start to become natural behavior. Being genuine and consistent is the key to reaching the lost. This isn't a hit or miss project. It requires patience and diligence, like most things in God's economy.

As we reflect on the different the types of people we encounter in our daily lives we come to realize that there are a wide variety of people we have to deal with. Many profess to know God; others do not. Some folks 'talk the walk', but don't 'walk the talk'. Some are familiar with the Christian 'jargon' and play the part, all the while not believing a word they're saying. Some, out of ignorance, blame God for every bad thing that has ever happened to them. Some, not understanding their current standing with God, simply don't want to discuss it. And that is just the tip of the iceberg.

The more I watch the news, the more I realize there are a whole lot of personality types I just can't relate to. I can't relate to those who drink beer until they fall down. I remember doing that once during my college days. Looking back at that time in my life I can't imagine would have done it then, so it stands to reason that I certainly can't imagine why anyone else would do it now. I *can*, however, relate to those who have been divorced, having experienced that mess not once, but twice. I can't relate to addictive personalities, but I *can* relate to people who have at one time had large incomes only to lose them quite suddenly. I can't relate to murderers in the least, but I *can* relate to people who have felt the sting of life's little (or sometimes big) injustices. I can't relate to the loss of a child, but I *can* relate to someone who has experienced the sudden and unexpected loss of a parent since I lost my mother to cancer when she was only 53 years old. I may not be able to relate to all situations people are going through, but someone can and God is wise enough to put those two individuals together to bring comfort and peace to that one who is suffering.

We don't always have to talk to someone to make an impact on him or her. I remember reading a story about Dwight D. Eisenhower visiting Sir Winston Churchill at London's King Edward VII Hospital as the latter was near death. Nary was a word spoken between the two men; Eisenhower simply sat there holding Churchill's hand for what is said to have been 10 minutes in complete silence. While nothing was ever said, I'm sure it meant a lot to Churchill to know that his dear friend cared enough to stop by. I share that story to say this: sometimes the greatest blessings come in silence.

Who Are We?

Perhaps Christians seem like a threat to non-believers because we know *whose* we are and that has a pronounced effect on *who* we are. When we are a child of God, we are His and He is ours and we know it. This breeds a certain confidence that the world doesn't have. Christians allow God to infiltrate their lives. It affects the way we think, speak and act. Non-believers don't have that relationship in their lives. They may believe in the existence of God, but have not seen the necessity of submerging themselves into an intimate, personal relationship with Him.

I think non-believers in large part don't really know who they are. They try to be somebody they aren't to fit into a group of their peers at school or work or in their neighborhood. Sometimes I think a lot of individuals embellish their accomplishments just shy of falsifying information when they interact with others because they want to be accepted as a means of fitting in. Christians do it just like non-Christians do. Apparently none of us have ever quite understood that God doesn't care what style clothes we wear, what car we drive, how much money we have; God cares about what's in our hearts. It's the same for all of mankind; knowing Christ establishes in us our worth.

Christians aren't exempt from not knowing who they are. Sometimes we feel lost in a sea of expectations and disappointments. We aren't as close to God as we know we need to be and as a result become guilt ridden, frustrated and disillusioned. We must be reminded that we are of immeasurable value to our Creator. We all must see not just sinners but also ourselves the way God sees us. Forgiveness doesn't make us any better off than the non-believer if we don't allow it to change us on the inside. True, we are bound for heaven, but our lives are a shadow of what they can be. If we roll in the mud and take a shower only to go roll in the mud again, what have we gained? As Christians, we must allow ourselves to be that new creation scripture talks about in 2 Corinthians 5:17; then extend the same grace to non-believers and even fellow believers that has been shown to us.

How can we relate to the unredeemed people around us or the less than committed church people who sit in our pews each Sunday morning? By being who God made us to be, warts and all. As I said earlier, the key lies in the genuineness and consistency of our behavior. We are who we are and God has declared it to be good. We need to work hard at our relationship with God and ask Him to enable us to be Jesus to those all around us. We *are* different than those that live in this world and that's okay. We have something they need and we need to present it to them in a patient, loving, relevant way. God knows how. We must listen to His Holy Spirit to find out what we are to do. Flying by the seat of our pants is not an option. Our walk with God is a process; it takes time. We want everything to take place when *we* think it should take place, but that isn't how it works with God. Everything takes time.

Have you ever considered that time is meaningless to God. He created time. He alone knows when time began and it will continue until He stops the clock from ticking. God also knows when the proper time is for certain things to take place. We get all crazy because in our impatience we think things are taking too long; however, God has made us a promise ... He *"works all things for the good of those who love Him and are called according to His purposes"* (Romans 8:28).

Being Merciful

Tragedy tends to draw people together. School shootings, devastating storms, untimely deaths all seem to draw out the best from people. We help neighbors we've never spoken to before and even assist total strangers in need. Our hearts go out to people who have lost everything. We don't see color or ethnicity, all we see are people suffering. If we can't relate, we can certainly empathize. It doesn't take much to envision our own lives thrown into chaos by cataclysmic events. In times such as these whole churches open their doors to help feed and clothe those in desperate need. We put our prejudices aside for the moment and we all become God's hand extended. What keeps us from being that way all the time? Some churches *do* feed the poor and clothe those less fortunate on a regular basis and that is to be highly commended. They are being Jesus to the community in which they live. Unfortunately, far too often once the calamity has passed we go back to our old ways. As mentioned in an earlier chapter, we have the severe problem of looking at the outer package and by that make our assessment as to whether the person is worthy of knowing. As followers of Christ we need to remember and not forget how God saw us prior to our conversion and how He sees us now. Have we lost sight of the mercy God extended to us?

Those that ridicule us for our beliefs don't understand their own need of forgiveness. The mere mention of the name Jesus makes them uncomfortable. Frankly, they really don't know any better than to make fun of that which they don't understand. I say nothing to unsaved people who drink around me, nor do I chastise them for cursing. Why; because these things are not heaven or hell issues. I drank and cussed like a fool before I knew Christ. How did God see me? He saw me through eyes of love and mercy. How could I do any different to those unsaved in my midst? How could any of us? God looks upon the heart. What have we accomplished if we criticize anyone for drinking or cussing? God accepts us the way we are and if we submit to the work of the Holy Spirit we slowly change from within. That's God's job, not ours.

The Luncheon

Our church had a special luncheon for people who were affected by Hurricane Sandy. Although it was three full months since the devastating storm some people were still going without bare necessities. Our Pastor had 1000 flyers sent out to a specific area we had earmarked to help. Approximately 40-45 people showed up at our fellowship hall for a nice lunch and any supplies they needed. The people were supremely appreciative of the assistance. We got to hug them, talk to them, pray with them and promise them they would not be forgotten by us. Several folks have begun to attend our church, but that was not at all the point of the whole exercise. The point was to meet the needs of those who were suffering.

This brings me to the following story. A friend of mine and I were sitting at a round table with some of the area folks. One gentleman came and sat down with us ... for the sake of the story we'll call him Bill. He looked to be in his 60's. Knit cap on his head, couple days growth of beard on his face, slightly jumbled teeth, several layers of winter clothes ... he was disheveled and a little on the dirty side. Now a first impression might be that he was an undesirable person; one who couldn't be trusted. God knows his heart. It appeared that he may have come simply for the food because he took no supplies, yet ate like there was no tomorrow. You know what, that was okay. He rattled on about his situation in rapid-fire fashion, so much so that it was a little hard to follow him. He told the same story to just about anyone that would listen. The curious thing to me was that while most seemingly unchurched people will usually show respect for the church with regards to their language, Bill let F-bombs and GD's and JC's fly at will ... didn't even flinch. I wasn't offended. His apparent disregard for his surroundings was interesting to me. He was a human being and was obviously hurting although he was trying very hard to keep from letting it show. You saw it in his eyes. My friend and I engaged him in conversation like we would anyone else. I have no idea what this man's story was; no idea where he was born, where he went to school, if he had siblings, if his parents were alive, what type of life he had had. I looked at him and saw a weary man who was trying to represent himself in the most positive way possible. Who was I to judge him; I don't know anything about him. He didn't want to leave any contact information so we bid him well telling him to please contact the church office if he needed anything else and we would do our best to help him. I hope he does. I hope we made him feel comfortable. I hope he saw God in us. He was uncomfortable being at a church, that was for sure, but I'm glad he came. I'm glad they all came. God loves Bill, just like He loves you and me. There are a lot of folks just like Bill in this world. It's our responsibility to be Christ to all the Bill's of the world.

Priorities

I believe there is a chain of command in God's economy and it goes something like this: God first, family second, others third and we bring up the rear. Putting yourself second, third or fourth in the priority line is unnatural and difficult to do. It's what is expected of us as believers and is in direct conflict with what the world preaches. God is to be number one in our lives, even above ourselves. We did not create ourselves and therefore must surrender our will to our creator. We are to be obedient and subservient to our God. In surrendering we must understand that we'll not get short changed. God promised to take care of us, so if God is providing for and sustaining us, that frees us up to do the same for others.

A lot of people, especially men, get uncomfortable when the topic of feelings and emotions comes up. We were created with emotions. We should relax and just be ourselves; however, society dictates that we act a certain way, dress a certain way, earn a certain amount and live a certain way. Anything short of that is considered out of the ordinary or abnormal. Rules of acceptability, set up by man, compartmentalize us so that we become nothing more than livestock. Those who feel compelled to keep up with all the latest trends don't allow their own uniqueness to shine through. God made each one of us as individuals, yet so many of us allow ourselves to be led into our social pens to graze with all the rest of the livestock that shirks originality. Being yourself is shunned; being a clone of those who are trendy and 'in' is desirable.

How can a Christian relate to all this without being caught up in it? It requires wisdom, patience and discernment. We are children of the King and have nothing to be embarrassed or ashamed of. God knows how to relate to those He puts us in contact with. As we grow in the grace and knowledge of Christ and let His Holy Spirit guide us we will find ways to relate to any given situation. That may sound like a pretty simplistic approach, but face it, God knows all that needs to be known about any given individual or situation and we do not. Perhaps we are unable to relate because we are attempting to do all this relating on our own. We won't become relatable by behaving like others. We will be relatable because God is relatable; *we* get in His way. We need to stand aside and let Him take the lead. Spending time with God is the only way we can know Him and be more like Him. There's no other way. As we become more like Christ what we say regarding our faith will come across as natural; like flowing water.

We Are All the Same to God

Everyone has a story. They haven't always been who they are standing before you today. They were once someone's child. Somewhere along the way they ran into a bad set of circumstances and perhaps made a poor choice that sent them down a dark path that they have been unable to return from. If it were you would you want to be judged or shown mercy? We are called by God to meet needs, to be a friend to the friendless, show compassion and understanding when it is lacking. Providing a meal for someone is a wonderful, thoughtful act of loving kindness, but what will they eat tomorrow or next week?

Homeless people, strippers, drug addicts, alcoholics; society has painted them in an unfavorable light and we shun them as a result. They don't fit into the mold society deems as normal. But they are also God's children; they have just lost their way. They need hope. They need love. Perhaps they need help standing on their own two feet again. We need to see all people the way God sees them; not just see the ones we deem worthy of being seen. *All* people have value in the eyes of God. Why would *we* see them any different? How did God look upon us? With disdain? With disgust? No. He looked at us with loving, merciful eyes and said "Come to me, all of you who are weary and carry heavy burdens, and I will give you rest." (Matthew 11:28)

The great thing about God is that He takes us where we stand just the way we are and holds us in His warm, loving, merciful arms. Clean or dirty, smelly or not … God loves us! How do we relate to those who are unlike us? They are loved by God just as we are. Human touch is healing. A kind word is a balm that can mend a broken heart. God has given us the ability to rehabilitate a sin sick and dying world. To relate to those around us we simply need to be who God made us to be and be that way with a genuine consistency. We don't need to compromise our beliefs, just *be* everything God knows we can be and allow His Holy Spirit to flow through us as we live our lives for Him.

People seem to have a certain perception of what a Christian is. They think a Christian is a churchgoer; but that's what a Christian does. They think a Christian doesn't smoke, drink or cuss; but those things don't make a person a Christian any more than an American living in Germany makes them a German. In a nutshell, a Christian is a person who is forgiven and under the umbrella of God's grace. What we *do* is an outpouring of what has been placed in our heart by God.

So what have we learned, if anything, about being relatable to those around us? We must embrace our uniqueness. God made us the way we are. We are to be the genuine article; there must be no falseness in us. Our walk and talk need to mesh so as not to be a contradiction of one another. John 12:32 says that if Christ is lifted up He will draw all men to Himself. Lift Christ up in your daily life.

"Everyone may not be good, but there's always something good in everyone. Never judge anyone shortly because every saint has a past and ever sinner has a future."

Oscar Wilde

CHAPTER 11

Consequences

"'I have the right to do anything,' you say—but not everything is beneficial. 'I have the right to do anything'—but not everything is constructive." (1 Corinthians 10:23)

Paul had a specific purpose for writing to the Corinthians. The Corinthian believers were becoming arrogant over their spiritual security and Paul needed to set them straight. As The Asbury Bible Commentary rightly points out; "Christian liberty unchecked may deteriorate into license and endanger not only the weak but the strong Christian as well."

The idea of consequences isn't relegated only to the New Testament. Nine times in the Old Testament [25] the word 'consequence(s)' is used. Each time it's referring to the result of the sins of the people of Israel or of an individual Israelite. Whether an individual believes in God or not, consequences shall come upon them, just as they shall come upon us all.

The truth revealed in verse 23 should not be considered a Biblical truth alone, but rather a universal truth. While it's true that we can do anything we want, not everything we do will be beneficial or constructive for either ourselves or those we love. In reality, this concept has nothing to do with God, for even if He *didn't* exist, there would still be consequences as the result of our words, actions and reactions. Every choice we make in this life has resulting consequences. Even inaction has consequences. We can't escape them; they are inevitable.

Consequences as a universal law are rooted in Newton's Third Law of Motion, which is: *"For every action, there is an equal and opposite reaction."*[26] If you throw a ball at a wall, it will come back to you, only faster. That is a result of physics. Consequences come from saying or doing something, whether right or wrong and having the results of those words or actions unfold. If you shoot a gun at a person, the consequences are that you will either kill them, injury them or miss them altogether (with the latter two the consequences are that you'll only be arrested for *attempted* murder.). If you run directly in front of a truck you'll get hit and either injured or killed. If you jump over Niagara Falls you'll drown. If you punch a police officer you'll go to jail. If you eat the wrong foods you'll gain weight. If you don't brush your teeth you'll get cavities and your breath will stink. If you don't eat all day you'll be hungry. Consequences are tied to pretty much everything we say and do.

God's Payment System

By definition, consequences are the result of a condition. The condition we all suffer from is sin. Sin is disobedience to God's standard set forth in the Bible. It has been established and written down by His own hand in the form of the Ten Commandments.

> *"The law is only a shadow of the good things that are coming—not the realities themselves. For this reason it can never, by the same sacrifices repeated endlessly year after year, make perfect those who draw near to worship. Otherwise, would they not have stopped being offered? For the worshipers would have been cleansed once for all, and would no longer have felt guilty for their sins. But those sacrifices are an annual reminder of*

sins. It is impossible for the blood of bulls and goats to take away sins." (Hebrews 10:1-4)

God set up a payment system for those who were disobedient. The payment requires the shedding of blood. These sacrifices could never erase the sins of the one making the sin offering; but rather, the sacrifice stood as an annual reminder of their sin. God created animals for man's use, yet some folks simply cannot accept a God that would be so cruel as to kill innocent animals. Have you ever considered, by means of comparison, what He allowed to happen to His own Son?

There was a purpose for each event in history that has taken place just as there is a reason for what takes place now. I don't pretend to know the mind of God in all matters; I just know that things happen in life and we don't know all the details. There are facts that are unknown to us. All we know is what the history books tell us and the media spoon-feeds us. I *do* know this though; it's a messy, bloody world we live in. Things that are wrong are made to seem right and vice versa. Sins are committed against God every day and the ultimate consequence of those sins is death unless a blood sacrifice is made on behalf of the offender. That blood sacrifice was made when Jesus Christ willingly shed His own blood to cleanse all of mankind of their sins. It must be understood that forgiveness isn't freely doled out to everyone arbitrarily; we must ask for forgiveness in faith believing to be cleansed.

There is no doubt that Christ was a lightning rod for controversy during His life and still is today. Could it be because His teachings contradicted the teachings of the religious leaders of His day? When you deal with people you are dealing with egos, control and power. Jesus was stripping some of that away from the religious leaders and they took exception to it; so much so that they wanted Him dead. That seems like an extreme way to rid themselves of their perceived problem. They didn't think about the consequences that would result from Christ's death. Christ knew exactly what the consequences were as a result of His obedience to God's plan. They spelled death for Him. The disobedience of all mankind was to be removed by the obedience of one man. Man's disobedience resulted in millions of sins down through the ages past and present. The weight of these sins must have been enormous. I feel heaviness from the weight of conviction for one sin that I hadn't yet sought forgiveness for; can you imagine the heaviness Christ felt when He hung on the cross?

The life that we choose to live on this earth is essentially what we make it. We can take a good path or a bad path. We can skate along the fine line that differentiates legal from illegal, right and wrong. We can live Godly lives or follow the path to who knows where. Each decision we make in this life comes with consequences.

Reaping & Sowing

"Do not be deceived: God cannot be mocked. People reap what they sow. Those who sow to please their sinful nature, from that nature will reap destruction; those who sow to please the Spirit, from the Spirit will reap eternal life." (Galatians 6:7-8)

"... the way one lives will undoubtedly be recognized by God as a true indication of what one is." [Asbury Bible Commentary]

"Now it is the hour of decision. Now his readers must consider very carefully the consequences of choosing one way or the other. They cannot drift; they cannot remain neutral;

they must decide whether they are going to walk by the Spirit or gratify the desires of their sinful nature." "Paul introduces his call for decision with a solemn warning based on an agricultural principle: Do not be deceived: God cannot be mocked. A man reaps what he sows (v. 7). When people think and act as if they will not reap what they have sown, or as if they will reap something different from what they have sown, they are deceiving themselves and mocking God. But since the inexorable law of reaping what is sown has always been proved true, the proverbial statement of warning God cannot be mocked is also true: no one can mock God and get away with it." [The InterVarsity Press New Testament Commentary Series]

Illustration: Planting Corn

Reaping and sowing is God's version of consequences. Here we have an example of what is entailed to reap a healthy crop of corn. When a farmer plants his crops, there is a certain procedure he must go through. He religiously follows this procedure so as to reap a plentiful crop. The following is a seven step plan for planting any type of seeds with the desired result sought being a healthy crop:

1) Choose the Right Spot
2) Prepare the Soil
3) Rake in the Fertilizer
4) Plant Seeds In the Ground
5) Water as Needed
6) Maintain the Seeds; weeds, pests
7) Harvest Your Crop [27]

What can we learn from the above planting procedure? When scripture tells us that we shall reap what we sow we need to do what another scripture tells us: *'count the cost'*. (Luke 14:28-30) There is a cost associated with following Christ and that cost isn't monetary. That cost is associated with the life we sow and the time spent with God and helping others. The seven steps laid out above help us see all that is entailed in growing a crop of corn. It is no different with the path we choose in life. Each life decision is like a seed sown in the earth. Our own relationship with Christ is a seed sown as well. The only way to reap the reward of a sound future or a fulfilling relationship with God is to cultivate it as you would the corn seeds mentioned above. Without the proper care the crop will wither and die, just as anything we undertake in life; whether it's our marriage, our relationship with our children, our career or our spiritual life.

Heaven and Hell

There is a certain order of things in the world. We are born and we die; in the middle of that is our life. What we do with it is completely up to us. It's like taking a blank canvas and different color paints and putting on that canvas whatever we want. Some peoples' lives are bright and cheerful, some are dark and brooding; the consequences of our own decisions.

Just as life has consequences, life also has rules. Some are common sense, some are voted on, some are simply laws of nature and some are generally accepted rules of ethics and personal conduct. The standard that has stood the test of time is the one constructed by Almighty God. We can debate about whether God exists or not until the end of time. It's a personal choice that we all must make at some point in our lives. I made the decision to live for God when I was 24 years old. Some make that choice on their deathbed. Regardless of when the decision is made, it's one that must be dealt with. It's our greatest and most difficult choice for in it lies our eternal destination.

Do we simply die and rot in a wooden box in the ground or do we spend an eternity after our death someplace else? Christianity teaches us of heaven and hell. Heaven is a place where God and His angels reside and where those who have accepted God's gracious offer of salvation will dwell for all eternity. Hell is the place that in Hebrew is referred to as Sheol or the abode of the dead. In Jewish thought it is believed to be the very deepest point under the earth; the point that is said to be the greatest distance from heaven. [28]

The Bible is very precise on the matter of who may avail themselves of salvation. 2 Peter 3:9 says *The Lord is not slow in keeping his promise, as some understand slowness. Instead he is patient with you, not wanting anyone to perish, but* **everyone** *to come to repentance.* God is patient and kind, but when time has ended and the period of judgment begins, there will be no acceptable excuses that God will entertain. The consequences of a life frittered away with wasted time and meaningless motion is eternal separation from God. A life lived for oneself and oneself only is no life at all, but rather a selfish, self-centered existence that has its' own set of consequences. Nothing escapes God's ever-watchful eye. He knows the true heart of an individual. Thinking we can live a life that makes a mockery of all God stands for and then waltz into heaven as if God saw nothing of the life we've lived is ludicrous. It's impossible to fool God. You can pull the wool over the eyes of all of creation your entire life, yet when you stand before God on the last day, you will be nothing more than a stammering fool. When scripture says God cannot be mocked you can believe it. The seeds you have sown during this life shall produce a crop that matches the attention that was given to its growth. Many a person has made a commitment to Christ only to let it wither away and turn to dust; the consequences of missed opportunities to live for God.

People see God in many different ways. They don't want to believe that He would actually keep anyone from entering into heaven so in their own minds they do not consider the notion of hell to be real. To some He's benevolent, to others a harsh judge. Some believe a certain way without scriptural substantiation; it's more of a gut feeling for them. The scriptures are clear who God is and how He operates. Those who refuse to believe are too busy concentrating on themselves to see.

Living for God

When I say 'live for God', I am speaking of when we enter into a relationship with God. It is then that the Holy Spirit enters us and begins making alterations from the inside out. If we spend any time at all in God's word we will begin to grow spiritually; the same happens if we start to attend a church of our choosing. As we grow we learn more about the things of God and what is required of us as His children and His ambassadors. *That* is what living for God means in a nutshell. It requires attention, patience, diligence, perseverance, faith, trust and determination, among other things. Regardless of our background or skill set, God wants to use us. Through ages past He has used those that are the least talented, least gifted to do the greatest work for His kingdom. Humility is the key; notoriety is irrelevant.

Living for God to me is utilizing the gift of writing I believe He's given me. I have no desire to become wealthy or famous. All I want to do is make a difference in people's lives one person at a time. In doing so I believe I will bring glory and honor to God. I trust Him to provide enough finances for me to afford to continue to publish my writing. The world cannot relate to that way of thinking. Some folks are so far removed from Godly living that they find it to be a bizarre way of life; too restrictive. They are ignorant to the truth and have accepted the lie of Satan that they can live as they choose with no adverse or negative consequences resulting from it. They have set up their own standards; however standards that do not work for all cannot be valid because while we are all individuals, we are all inextricably connected. The common bond is Almighty God, for He created each one of us.

In this sad, dreary, scary world we live in, hope can be hard to find; however, hope can blossom from our actions and/or reactions. A kind word or compliment can bring a smile. A helping hand or small act of kindness blesses the recipient. Money given without any repayment sought, prayers said on behalf of someone in need, providing food for a struggling family … these are all examples of things that bring positive consequences. It just so happens that they all plant seeds as well. Seeds of peace, comfort and hope planted in the name of Christ. There are so many other good things that we do in the name of Jesus that bring contentment, comfort and hope to those less fortunate then us. It's being Christ to those around us. It's stepping out of our self-constructed comfort zones and meeting a crucial need at just the right time. God wants to use us. All we need is a willing heart. If we know God meets all our needs, then we should reach out to those who need a touch from God. The consequences are never bad when we operate in the realm of the spirit. When we obey God's leading and follow through we get blessed too. Always remember and never forget, as I've said before, it's never right to do the wrong thing and conversely, it's never wrong to do the right thing.

Life's Harsh Reality

One of the difficult consequences that we all must deal with at one point or another in our lives is death. It is one of life's harsh realities.

Speaking of God to a person who just lost the love of his life to cancer requires much silent consolation, as well as being spirit led. Believers and non-believers alike want to know at a time like that where God is and why He allowed it to happen. Unfortunately, the only answer one can give sometimes is that 'death is a part of life'. It seems like a cold, heartless thing to say, but it's the obvious truth. It isn't anyone's fault and we don't want to hear it, but it doesn't make it any less true. People live and people die. It's a consequence of life. When my mom died at 53 years of age I didn't want to hear anything from anybody. It's only later on down the road that I was able to make any sense of her death at all. I still don't know why she had to die, but I believe in my heart that she is with God and that made it all right for me.

Death is the natural progression in one's life; it comes to us all. Those that know God have nothing to fear. Those who don't believe there is a God have much to fear. Fear is a feeling of anxiety or apprehension regarding an impending event or event that *may* take place in the future; we fear the unknown. It's the fear some feel when they go into a pitch-dark room. The first thing they do is grope for a light switch.

There is nothing in this life that we can do to ward off death. God brings us into this life and ushers us out. It's the natural cycle of life that we all must go through. The consequences that we must either endure or enjoy are a direct result of the choices we make in this life.

Some choose to live a solitary life, devoid of responsibilities except to themselves and their own interests. To those individuals, I give them a portion of Anglican poet & clergyman John Donne's Meditation XVII. We are not alone, in spite of how we may feel and life is not all about *'me'*.

> *"All mankind is of one author, and is one volume; when one man dies, one chapter is not torn out of the book, but translated into a better language; and every chapter must be*

so translated…As therefore the bell that rings to a sermon, calls not upon the preacher only, but upon the congregation to come: so this bell calls us all: but how much more me, who am brought so near the door by this sickness…No man is an island, entire of itself…any man's death diminishes me, because I am involved in mankind; and therefore never send to know for whom the bell tolls; it tolls for thee." [29]

Donne deals with two ideas here: one of isolation and one of mortality. The idea of man being isolated and to himself is dismissed as he alludes to man being interconnected. We all come from one God and are therefore forever intertwined with one another. Death walks stride for stride with life as its constant companion. It's always present in that we are always aware of its eventuality. The consequences of living an isolated life are that we live presuming that there is no connection to our fellow man. This would be true if there were no God. Isolation is the product of ignorance and a stubborn constitution that doesn't allow for new thoughts or concepts to be pondered and possibly accepted as true.

If we've learned anything from this chapter we have learned that consequences can come in many different forms; sometimes good, sometimes bad. They are tied to the words or actions we have taken. They are unavoidable. Right life decisions breed good consequences. Allowing God to lead us through life will cause us to achieve in our heart of hearts what we truly desire; peace, joy and hope for the future.

"I have learned from experience that the greater part of our happiness or misery depends on our dispositions and not on our circumstances."

Martha Washington

CHAPTER 12

Vulnerability

Dr. Brené Brown recently wrote a book dealing with the topic of vulnerability [30]. In the book she debunks three myths regarding this topic. Let's touch on them briefly.

The first one is that *"vulnerability is weakness"*. She describes vulnerability as the core of all emotions; something that helps us connect with others. *"It opens us up to love, joy, creativity and empathy,"* says Brown. Here are some examples she lists that could make us vulnerable: *"starting your own business; calling a friend whose child just passed away; trying something new; getting pregnant after having three miscarriages; admitting I'm afraid; having faith."* As we express our inner most thoughts and fears we become vulnerable to the criticism of others. It takes courage to speak the truth and that opens us up to judgment, yet it is anything but weak.

The second myth is that some do not experience vulnerability. Dr. Brown says that *"life is vulnerable"* so if we are alive, it stands to reason, based on her statement that vulnerability is inescapable. We have no choice whether we are vulnerable or not. According to Brown, *"the choice is how we respond when the elements of vulnerability greet us: uncertainty, risk and emotional exposure."*

The third myth is that *"vulnerability means spilling your secrets."* Feeling vulnerable doesn't mean that we have to spill our guts to anyone and everyone who will listen but rather only to those we trust.

"Vulnerability is about sharing our feelings and our experiences with people who have earned the right to hear them," says Brown.

The Uniqueness of You

God created our personalities and made us totally unique; one of a kind. When we try to hide our vulnerability it masks our true identity. Our inner most thoughts and feelings are who we are as a person; however, we needn't spill our deepest, innermost thoughts to anyone who comes along. That should be reserved for the special people in our lives like spouses, siblings, parents or close friends.

Those that appear or act differently than others are considered abnormal or weird. Society determines what is acceptable and what isn't. Flying in the face of that is the fact that Jesus sees us all the same, regardless of our outward appearance. We must remember that our bodies are nothing more than a temporary housing for our soul and spirit. When we pass from this earth our body decays, returns to dust and is no more. So why do we put such a high premium on the outward appearance? I'm not sure, but we have been conditioned to do so and it's an impedance to loving and serving others in the name of Christ.

As a side note, I have yet to find a proper definition for normalcy. 'Normal' depends on who is accessing the behavior in question. My normal is different than your normal that is different than another's normal and so on. People are not weird, they are simply different than we are and generally speaking that doesn't make them weird. Perhaps calling someone weird shines a light on our own sense of inadequacy. They are free to display their total personality, being who God created them to be and we are uncomfortable with that.

Being Vulnerable to Non-believers

As Christians, the more we intermingle with non-Christians, the more we expose ourselves to the ignorance of others. We leave our tender white underbellies exposed, in a manner of speaking. If we are in a relationship with Christ and not just playing church, then we need to allow ourselves to be vulnerable, for it may be the only way to reach some folks. It may mean not flinching when someone drops multiple F-bombs or other colorful language in a conversation. Let's be honest with ourselves; haven't we all dropped an F-bomb or two or let something you wouldn't typically say slip out when angry or frustrated. I know I have. That doesn't make it okay, but it also won't revoke our entrance into heaven. I must clarify though that an occasional slip means you're human, but used repeatedly as if it were acceptable speech is absolutely not okay. Either way repentance is necessary.

Because non-believers drink, smoke and swear doesn't mean they are the devils spawn. It means they are different than we are. God won't keep them out of heaven because they drink, smoke and swear or worse. God will keep them out of heaven because they have rejected Christ and the forgiveness He freely provides for them. That's it and that's all. Once saved God will root out the things that are displeasing to Him by His Holy Spirit if He is allowed to. It's a progressive thing that has everything to do with how much time and effort we put into our personal relationship with God. He makes these alterations in His own time and in His own way changing us from the inside out. That's the same thing He did with you and me. Isn't it funny how quickly we forget how we were before we knew Christ? It should be noted that those who are newly saved yet have done things that require punishment will still need to suffer the consequences of their actions; however, their soul is clean and the sins are washed away.

Allowing ourselves to be vulnerable by befriending others helps show them we care. We are at a distinct disadvantage because people tend to be leery of us when they find out we are 'born again' to begin with. I prefer to break the ice with people by telling them I believe in God and in the power of prayer. If that provides an opening, I continue by saying I believe we can have a personal relationship with God. It's nothing more than a matter of semantics, yet doesn't have such a negative stigma attached to it. The unsaved don't know our jargon so we must allow the Spirit to flow through us and begin to massage their heart.

Becoming a friend who stays in touch will show them we are not just performing a hit and run. Helping people shouldn't be done just when it's convenient for us. It may be very inconvenient at times, like when they are in distress and we are in the middle of something we consider important. We may just need to climb out of our comfort cave and help meet a need of theirs. Being friends with an unsaved individual for the sake of winning them to Christ alone is disingenuous. Yes, we care about the condition of their soul, but hitting them square between the eyes with the gospel may not be the best approach. It depends on who they are and what their story is. Letting God have the lead is imperative because He already knows them. When dealing with any interpersonal relationship, genuineness and honesty are critical. People must feel they can trust us. The Holy Spirit at work *in* us will be what draws others *to* us. It's not play-acting. As we draw closer to God He will draw closer to us (James 4:8) and changes will take place within our heart. Unbelievers need what God has to offer and we are the ones God has chosen to make the presentation. We just need to be real about it.

Bad Examples

I've known ministers who have been right at your side sharing the good news of the gospel every day and then become like a phantom once you receive Christ. If they are the head of a ministry, they probably leave the follow-up to their assistants. The problem is that a bond has been made with the head of the ministry. At one college campus ministry I saw some new converts drift away because they had become close to the leader and then, all of a sudden, he was unavailable to them even when they were in distress. That isn't good because the assistants are fellow students who were ill prepared to handle many of the questions the new converts had. Leaders should always try to be somewhat available, with the understanding that they have a whole group of people they are responsible for. When we are dealing with people's feelings and emotions we need to be considerate and empathetic. Some people will be hurt or offended no matter how you handle yourself or what you say to them. We can only control our own words and actions, not those of others. One approach to this type of scenario might be for the leader to introduce the new converts to a particular student leader to act as a mentor, rather than simply leaving the newbie to find them on their own.

We also need to be aware of sponges. These types of people seem to *always* have a problem and *never* take any of our advice. I use absolute terms like 'always' and 'never' because I have known a few people who were exactly like that. They didn't want help; they just wanted to talk to you in person or on the phone until your ear melted off the side of your head. I knew one fella who had the ministry's directory and called every number right down the line until he got a hold of someone. No "hello" or "this is so and so" … he just barged full steam into his diatribe, never caring if the person on the other end was listening or not. When they either hung up on him or ended the call in some fashion he moved on to the next name on the list. Now I would never advocate being rude or insensitive to anyone; however, some people will sap your time endlessly if you let them. There is no help for them because they don't really want help; they just want to complain about anything and everything. They don't want assistance, money, bible verses or prayer. They just want to complain about how rotten their life is.

I was working the overnight shift by myself at a Christian radio station a number of years ago and this same fellow I mentioned in the above paragraph called the prayer line at the station. I recognized his voice instantly and couldn't believe it was him, of all people. Now it was close to the time when I had to go on the air and do the news, so I had limited time for him. I kept trying to tell him I had to go and he just kept talking. Finally I set the phone down on the table and walked away to prepare the newscast and then deliver it over the air. Roughly fifteen minutes later I picked up the phone again and he was still talking. He didn't even know there was no one listening on the other end. That's very sad. Some folks have convinced themselves that their lives are worse than anyone else's ever could be and no amount of counseling or prayer will help them if they are *that* closed minded.

Vulnerability Personified

As Christians, we make ourselves vulnerable by following the lead of our Lord. Jesus made Himself vulnerable in that He gave Himself up and endured brutal punishment for something He didn't do. He didn't fight back; He didn't call down warrior angels to wipe out his punishers. He could have done all that and more, yet He submitted to His punishment for our sake. He made Himself vulnerable to the point of death.

We haven't had to endure any physical persecution in the United States. While there may be exceptions to this, generally speaking the most we suffer for our faith is ridicule. Most of us know nothing of suffering for Christ's sake. In some countries people are killed for their beliefs or ostracized by their family. Some lose everything for the sake of Christ. Have you ever considered what you would do if it came to that in America some day?

We live in a material world that has presented society with so many palatable versions of God and Jesus that it makes your head spin. The true gospel many times gets lost in the sauce. So many follow ritualistic forms and traditions and don't know the first thing about a personal relationship with God; they more than likely don't even realize God is that approachable. They don't speak to others about God because they don't know *what* they believe or in some cases, *why* they believe. Life makes them a different kind of vulnerable. Vulnerable to the evil that permeates our world. Their vulnerability produces worry that leads to fear. They find no hope in their empty beliefs and wind up questioning the very existence of God in the end. Without God, there is no hope and no real future; at least none of any substance. When this type of vulnerability takes hold of a person, they are at risk of falling prey to the conmen and charlatans who only pretend to represent God. People need to use discernment and God provides that for us in the person of the Holy Spirit. Christ's vulnerability may be the example we are to follow; however, we must be careful not to be taken advantage of.

Invulnerability

It's interesting to me that while we are vulnerable to our surroundings, we serve a God who is just the opposite; He is <u>in</u>vulnerable. By definition, it is impossible to harm or damage God in any way. He is invincible; defined in scripture as being omnipotent or all-powerful. This is the reason why although we allow ourselves to be somewhat vulnerable to those around us for the sake of the kingdom; we are never truly and completely vulnerable because we serve an all-powerful God. There's nothing that can harm us in the world without God's permission and even then He has the entire situation under control at all times. As we go through our lives we can move with confidence, for God is on our side and is in us in the person of the Holy Spirit. As we learn from our Lord we find out how to move through life as He would have us move.

A Christian's life is not one of ritualistic boredom with a long list of do's & don'ts. A Christian's life can be as exciting as we decide to make it. Our walk *with* God must coincide with our talk *about* God. It does us no good and presents a poor example to those around us if our talk doesn't sync up to our walk. When we do that we then become what is said of us; we become hypocrites. As noted previously, this is a major complaint of non-Christians; that Christians are poor examples of God's love. It should be added that those who complain probably don't have the faintest notion what God's love even looks like. It's really nothing more than an excuse they use to not listen to us. We need to take that excuse away.

The Reality of Things

Let's get real here, shall we. In reality, we are all liars, hypocrites and thieves; every last one of us. We lie to ourselves all the time about our walk with God, believing that we are just fine when in reality we still have much growing to do. We pompously pound the gavel of righteousness while we daily wrestle with temptations. We steal time from God, our families and our employers constantly as we selfishly roll through life.

We are similar in many ways to the ones we are attempting to persuade. Perhaps if we admitted our vulnerability as well as our frailty and difficulty living the way God desires us to live we may get someone's attention.

Once we learn a little humility by realizing that we are truly nothing without Christ, maybe we will start to make some headway in the business of reaching lost souls. They don't want to be preached at; they want something that is real and alive. Our vulnerability can be a tool that speaks to the masses; both saved and unsaved. Some folks sit in the pews every Sunday but don't know the difference between the Old Testament and the New Testament. It's a personal deal. Not a 'hide-it-under-a-bushel' kind of personal, but rather personal as in individual. God can use our vulnerability as an advantage as we allow the Holy Spirit to fill us with boldness. Talk to people. Allow God to use you. We are conduits; vessels made for the master's use. The Lord will always use a willing vessel. Making ourselves available is the key. If we never go to any church functions, we won't know who our brothers and sisters in the congregation are. We can start by being a blessing to them. It all starts with baby steps. Regardless of who you are in the body of Christ, God wants to use you. There's a learning process. As we walk with God we become more in tune with His will. Christians are rarely seen as successful by the world, for their standards are based on a whole different set of rules. But if our hearts are pure before God and we listen to the still small voice of the Spirit, we will be successful in the eyes of God and isn't that really all we want as believers? I can honestly say that all I long to hear from my Savior when I enter into heaven are those blessed words: *"Well done, thou good and faithful servant: … enter into the joy of the lord."* (Matthew 25:21) What a blessed day that will be.

"In the beginning, people think vulnerability will make you weak, but it does the opposite. It shows you're strong enough to care."

Victoria Pratt, actress

CHAPTER 13

MINIMALISM & INDIVIDUALISM

"Minimalism is simply a tool to get rid of life's excess so you can focus on life's important things."

"It's a very self-revealing process and lifestyle. Once we begin to remove the distraction and clutter from our life, our minds are clear to dig deeper into our own heart and soul."[31]

"What Minimalism is really all about is reassessment of your priorities so that you can strip away the excess stuff – the possessions and ideas and relationships and activities – that don't bring value to your life."[32]

Most people down through the ages are like a bird making its nest; we bring things into our lives that make us feel comfortable and at peace. Things that bring stress are avoided at all costs. Minimalism is a lifestyle concept that points outward instead of inward and sidesteps the natural urge to accumulate. Without the inclusion of God you have simply another idea among a multitude of ideas that works for some folks and not for others. Plug God into the concept and you have something worth putting into practice. I personally agree with Minimalism in its rawest and most basic form. I have come to believe that simpler is better; less entanglements, less to manage and less to eat my time.

Minimalism, in and of itself, can be both positive and negative. It can be said that in one respect minimalism is the enemy of success. If we do as little as possible at anything, we will only achieve minimal success. In relation to the things of God, we can use whatever gifts God has given us for His glory or we can let them collect dust on the shelf. When we do just enough to get by we are cheating others and ourselves out of potential blessings from God.

The positive side of minimalism is the school of thought that deals with reassessment, which is a good thing. When someone becomes a Christian they should as a natural course of their new faith reassess what is and isn't important to them. It's important to allow the Holy Spirit to extract from our lives those things and people that hinder us in our walk with God. What we're doing is merely jettisoning baggage that weighs us down. It's a safe bet that's not what the Minimalists had in mind when they came up with their philosophy.

People also like to accumulate 'things' because it brings them some sense of satisfaction. It's done on impulse many times and has nothing to do with work, bills or problems of any sort. It's a hobby that gives us a mini escape from reality. There's not one single thing wrong with having a hobby of this nature as long as it doesn't lead to an obsession that drives a wedge in the relationship between you and God.

As a means of example I offer the following: I had a 1400 piece comic book collection that I had been accumulating since 1992. It was neatly packaged with backing boards in plastic sleeves all alphabetized; neat and orderly. I never looked at them, but was glad to have them. Every time I moved I had to tote all eight boxes of comics to my next place of residence. They were fairly heavy and as a result it was becoming a drag. After my last divorce I ended up leaving them in Texas. They had become a bit of a millstone around my neck. The same can be said of my ball card collection. I couldn't even tell you how many thousands of baseball, football, basketball and hockey cards I had. I even had a Dan Marino rookie card encased in 2 inch thick Lucite. I came to the conclusion after I left for New Jersey that all those things were just accumulated 'stuff'. It was fun for a while, but it was non-essential to my life, so I left them behind. What happens to them is really unimportant to me. I must admit, the decision to leave such things behind is always easier when you don't have room in your car upon leaving and you can't afford to drive 2600 miles back to retrieve them. In the light of that fact I came to the realization that while there was nothing at all wrong with collecting such things and nothing wrong with holding on to them, there comes a time in a person's life when they simply need to let go of some things. They had become dust catchers; space wasters that always seemed to be under foot. It was time to let them go. God gave me a peace about all that and I have no regrets.

The acquiring of things is one thing; however, in the end it *can* end up being a huge waste of time and money. The real issue in all this is if we have become so fixated on the accumulation of things that we lose our focus on what should matter most. Living for God is a daily life-altering experience that we cannot allow to be nudged aside by peripheral events or material possessions. Our spirit man cannot survive without drinking from the well that never runs dry (John 4:14), just as we can't physically survive without liquid and solid sustenance. Non-Christians don't understand this concept. Many have acquired the philosophy 'live and let live', never realizing how non-beneficial that way of thinking truly is.

The simplification of our lives doesn't mean that we need to discard *all* material possessions unless, of course, you feel strongly compelled to do so. Chances are you don't, so focus on the unnecessary items; those things that are collecting dust in the attic or basement. Please understand, having family heirlooms or personal keepsakes is not a sin. That isn't at all what I am talking about. The simplification process doesn't have to be complicated, nor does it have to bring with it sorrow. It can bring freedom if we simply release our accumulations to God and let the Holy Spirit help us sort it all out.

Minimalism in Evangelism

Let's take a look at a minimalist approach to evangelism. If Christians did as little as possible to present the gospel message to the world, how many people do you think would come to know Christ? By the same token, how much spiritual growth would we experience if we rarely read our Bible, didn't attend church and didn't pray? If we aren't walking close to God then we won't grow and will have virtually no positive impact for Christ. How would you like it if Jesus didn't go all the way to the cross, but rather changed his mind because He wasn't in the mood or didn't sense the urgency? Christianity would never have taken off and we would still be lost in our sins.

There's a battle going on in the Spirit Realm for the souls of men. Demons and Angels are in battle all the time, at times right in our midst. We don't see it because we don't live in their realm, but I believe it to be real. The devil is constantly trying to trip up believers with temptations and ungodly lures. We must strengthen ourselves for battle. We're told by Paul in his letter to the Ephesians to *"gird your loins with truth"* (Ephesians 6:14 NASB). In the plainest sense of the phrase it means to 'prepare to defend yourself'. This isn't a game. Souls are at stake and we are the vessels God has chosen to present His message to a lost and dying world. As our faith grows, so do our defenses against the enemy. Those that do little to further the kingdom of God are no threat to the enemy and so are pretty much left alone much of the time.

The devil is constantly trying to trip us up and make us ineffective. The only way to defend ourselves against the enemy is to fill our mind with the Word of God. This will have a trickle-down effect as the truth finds its way into our hearts and permeates our souls. We can ward off any and all danger if we defend ourselves with the truth of God. Our mission is to present that same truth to unbelievers as the Lord leads us. It's my assertion that we can never get too close to God. It can be said that even though He resides within the believer by His Spirit, we can still ignore Him. We need to practice listening. As we know the character of God better we will learn to discern that which is from Him versus that which is from the enemy or from our own mind. Even the staunchest believer can be fooled into thinking that something is so incredibly right, when waiting on God would have revealed that it was not right for them at all. A minimalist approach to our walk with God or our reaching out to the unsaved is of no use to the Lord. We must either be 'all in' or 'all out', there is no 'in between'. A slipshod application of our beliefs will benefit no one. Wearing a large silver or gold cross around our neck is no more than a fashion statement if we don't have a personal relationship with the One who hung on that cross. God wants us to maximize our efforts to electrify the world with His message of loving forgiveness. The only way we can accomplish that is to surrender our will over to God.

Self-Assessment

Do not merely listen to the word, and so deceive yourselves. Do what it says. Anyone who listens to the word but does not do what it says is like someone who looks at his face in a mirror and, after looking at himself, goes away and immediately forgets what he looks like. (James 1:22-24)

Self-assessment is very difficult for anyone. Only those serious about making alterations to their behavior will succeed. The Bible gives us excellent directives on how we should and shouldn't act in this life. We can always count on others to find our faults. The key is for us to find them and eradicate them with the Spirits help. The good thing about all this is that no matter what faults and flaws we may have, it doesn't put a damper on the way God feels about us. He loves us regardless of our flubs, foibles, insensitivities and lack of tact. As we walk with our Lord we can count on His Holy Spirit to draw to our attention all the things that need to be adjusted. We must allow this sort of spiritual surgery to take place. We can run just as Jonah did when God commissioned him to go preach salvation to the Ninevites (Jonah 1-4), but when we are finished running, God will be there waiting to draw us back to Himself. We might as well give in the first time and allow the surgery to commence. God knows it's for our benefit, even if we don't understand. That's what trusting in God is all about; relying on Him to show us where to go, when to go and what to say. God knows how to use us in a way that benefits us the most and brings Him the greatest glory.

Individualism: Defined

Individual – (adj.) single; separate; designed for use by one person; (noun) a single human being as distinct from a group, class, or family.

Individualism - the habit or principle of being independent and self-reliant; self-centered feeling or conduct; egoism.

Egoism or Egotism - an ethical theory that treats self-interest as the foundation of morality.

While we are all individuals and equal in the sight of God there is, like minimalism, a positive and a negative side to individualism. Man fancies himself as independent and self-reliant and he is to a certain extent. He is capable of fending for himself on a daily basis; providing a home, food for himself and if he has one, his family and so on. We all have a certain level of intellect that when used constructively serves us well. Remember John Donne's line? *"No man is an island, entire of itself; every man is a piece of the continent, a part of the main."* [33] The Apostle Paul echoes Donne's sentiments in his first letter to the Corinthians; *"For the body is not one member, but many."* (1 Corinthians 12:14)

It is understandable to think that the non-believer might consider himself an island unto himself. Without a god to seek assistance from the non-believer is on his own. Oh, there may be family or other individuals such as close friends who would come to his aid, but without God his resources are limited. In the church, we are not individuals or at least we aren't supposed to be. We are individuals in that we are unique, made that way by God; however, we function best as an entire body of believers. We are called a community and a family. We are not in it for fame and glory. We are in it for the greater good with God receiving all the glory. Individualism is the enemy of teamwork. In a sports setting how do you think a team would fare if each member played for himself and for his own statistical advancement? Not very well I'm afraid. With the team concept in mind, believers must bind together with other individuals to achieve the greatest good for the masses. We can reach many more with a team effort than with an individual effort.

1 Corinthians 12 talks about how the eye cannot function separate from the foot or from the ears. Our bodies function as one connected series of elements to accomplish various tasks. Each body part can do nothing on its own; they must all function together. Hospitals are filled

with folks whose bodies are not functioning properly. It serves as a living example of how things are when they don't work well together.

Egotism is another way of saying someone is self-absorbed. They are only concerned with what affects them directly or indirectly. Their moral compass is regulated by their own self-interest. They essentially devise their own standard to live by and ignore all other standards set before them.

The One Positive

The only positive I can come up with regarding being an individualist is that our relationship with God is accomplished on an individual basis. Blanket pardons aren't in play here. We sin as individuals and therefore we must seek forgiveness as individuals. My use of the word individualist may be contrary to the definition given; however, there is no doubting the fact that we serve an individual God who sent His individual Son to purchase redemption for mankind, one individual at a time.

We must understand that being an individual in Christ sets us apart from those in the world who side-step all religious affiliations, viewing them as unnecessary or some sort of crutch needed only by the weak. Some consider hell some sort of place where decadence rules and parties go on non-stop. I believe hell to be a very real place where those who turn their back on God entirely end up. Christianity can be broken down to this simple set of consequences: the consequence of sin is separation from God; the consequence of Christ shedding His blood is the forgiveness of sin; the consequence for sin being forgiven is that our separation from God has been bridged. That bridge is the cross.

We all sin; we can all be forgiven. It requires submission. Submission leads to commitment that leads to a relationship that leads to freedom that leads to peace that leads to fulfillment. We all have the right to choose. The great American Poet Robert Frost, not a Christian per se, but rather a Unitarian, put it this way: *"I hold it to be the inalienable right of anybody to go to hell in his own way."* An interesting statement from a man who had a wide range of rather jumbled and vague beliefs, yet didn't deny the existence of God.

Our 'No Touch' Society

The other day I was walking in the mall and I noticed something; nearly everyone I saw was either texting or talking on a cell phone. A thought crossed my mind: Is it possible we as a society have lost the art of interpersonal relations? We seem to no longer be individuals, but rather corporate puppets that buy the latest new thing and stay glued to it until the next new thing comes along. Have we gotten so caught up in new technology that we are now neglecting human touch for anything other than lustful pleasure? Christians have bought into the new techno wave as they too have laptops, kindles, iPads, iPhones, iPods and so on. We haven't gotten up to change the channels on our televisions in decades. Our collective eyes burn from hours of exposure to screens of all shapes and sizes. We have found a new addiction. Convenience is king. Delays are tragic. We have new generations being raised up that don't communicate in full sentences anymore. They don't think for themselves. They focus on nonessentials and leave things vital to a human's existence by the way side, like love, peace, patience, hope, mercy and forgiveness.

I feel the need to make a disclaimer so as not to be misunderstood. None of these technological marvels are evil in and of themselves. I too have a smart phone, iPod, laptop and kindle. I just don't let them rule my life, but rather use them as convenient tools to accomplish some of the necessities of life. I am simply saying that it seems to me our reliance on them has superseded our desire for the warmth of a mother's touch or the physical companionship of a friend or spouse. We, as a society, have become so addicted to texting that it's climbing the charts as a cause of multiple car accidents. I have seen so many young people paying half attention to the road as they speed past me at 70-80 mph texting with both hands as they go, displaying a 'nothing bad ever happens to me' type of attitude.

Okay, so what is really my point here? We serve a God who wants our full attention, not just lip service and a casual glance as we fiddle with our phones. He desires that we receive the full extent of His blessings. How can we ever hope to be Jesus to anyone if we don't look up from our iPad's long enough to see them? Texting is fine. Cell phones are fine. All the new technology is fine. And no, I am not saying that as if my word gives some sort of absolution. Perhaps I am mistaken, Lord knows I have been plenty of times before, but wouldn't our witness be much more effective and real if we did things in person with embracing and laughing and talking in real time with no electronic delays. Take advantage of the new wave of the latest and greatest communication tools, by all means, but don't do it to the exclusion of personal contact with those you are trying to reach for Christ and those you love.

Remember 1 Corinthians 10:23 – "'I have the right to do anything,' you say—but not everything is beneficial. 'I have the right to do anything'—but not everything is constructive." Do as you please, but know that whatever we say and do brings consequences. I'm not judging or condemning; just trying to get you to think.

"Only God who made us can touch us and change us and save us from ourselves."
Billy Graham

CHAPTER 14

WORDS

Word - speech as distinct from action.

"When we put bits into the mouths of horses to make them obey us, we can turn the whole animal. Or take ships as an example. Although they are so large and are driven by strong winds, they are steered by a very small rudder wherever the pilot wants to go. Likewise, the tongue is a small part of the body, but it makes great boasts. Consider what a great forest is set on fire by a small spark. The tongue also is a fire, a world of evil among the parts of the body. It corrupts the whole body, sets the whole course of one's life on fire, and is itself set on fire by hell." (James 3:3-6)

The Epistle of James is said to be, in part, how one is to order his life in keeping with a professed faith in God. The writer, understanding the true nature of the tongue and the words it produces, issues two illustrations regarding how something small in size can control something much larger. In the case of the horse, the bit goes in the mouth as part of the bridle that goes over their entire head. It is used as a means of controlling the animal's movements. In the case of a ship, the rudder is very small in comparison to the vessel itself, yet can easily control its movements. In each illustration it should be noted that the common denominator is that an individual is required to pull on the reins of the bridle or man the helm of the ship. In like manner, man has control of his tongue, or does he? He's supposed to and that is the point of the writer's comments.

There is no doubt that we can do much good with the words we say; however, we can also tear down a person's spirit with one negative statement. Words can bring healing and hope or depression and despair. Words can be a salve or a sword. Words.

> *"With the tongue we praise our Lord and Father, and with it we curse human beings, who have been made in God's likeness. Out of the same mouth come praise and cursing. My brothers and sisters, this should not be. Can both fresh water and salt water flow from the same spring? My brothers and sisters, can a fig tree bear olives, or a grapevine bear figs? Neither can a salt spring produce fresh water."* (James 3:9-12)

Our own ignorance causes us to say stupid things. With all the best intentions, we end up wounding someone's feelings or perhaps even crushing their spirit. Once these words are spoken they are "out there". They cannot be reeled back in as if they were attached to a fishing line. They can't be deleted as if they were typed out on a Word document on one's computer. They are hanging out there. Words, improperly used, can cause a lot of damage.

One of the things that is very dangerous about texting, online chatting, emailing, face booking and twittering is that our tone of voice is not always apparent. We can convey the wrong message without intending to if we are not careful. I once knew someone who texted everything in caps. I explained to her that using all caps in written form denotes to the reader excitement or upset. She insisted that I was wrong, naturally. That made her clueless to this social media faux pas.

> **Integrity** - the quality of being honest and having strong moral principles; moral uprightness; the state of being whole and undivided.

Tied to our words is our integrity. If we are careless with our words, we can have our personal integrity called into question. For the Christian our uprightness is crucial. We must understand that non-believers *will* take us to task for anything they feel is inappropriate behavior for someone who is supposed to be "religious". They wouldn't know any more what being a Christian entails than the man in the moon, but they never fail to miss an opportunity to challenge our behavior.

Just this weekend a non-believer made a point of my not going to church. It had been a long week that involved my driving from New Jersey to Atlanta, GA over to Savannah, GA and then back to Jersey again. I decided to take a break and was called out by a person who wouldn't darken the door of a church if their life depended on it. My response to her was "I assure you, God is not keeping attendance." Later this same woman challenged the fact that a Christian on Television had a tattoo. She said, "The Bible speaks out against that, doesn't it?" Fortunately, we are serving a gracious and merciful God and not all the various whims of a non-believer. God is loving, patient and kind to His children; the world is not; especially not when it comes to Christians. We are a threat to their order of things.

Words can mean something very different depending on how they are used. They can have duel meanings. The word 'gay' used to mean 'happy', now it means something totally different and as a result of its current meaning can tend to be somewhat polarizing. The phrase 'shut up' used to mean you were telling someone to be quiet in a somewhat harsh manner; now it can be a slang term for disbelief. Many words that children would get their mouths washed out with soap for saying are now accepted as normal English or urban slang. Someone somewhere decreed it to be so and it was so. Christianity provides order and stability; yet it is only seen as restrictive and demanding. It really all depends on your point of view and it logically all goes back to what your core beliefs are. The corruption of our entire language has made speech challenging. Ethnic groups seem to have their own self-constructed dialects that don't crossover into other ethnic groups. Instead of bridging cultural gaps that exist, we seem to be driving a wedge into the heart of our collective cultural consciousness. People don't seem to be able to communicate in person anymore; everything is done through smart phones or computers. Personal interaction is a thing of the past in many quadrants of our society. Now these are general assessments and not indicative of all economic strata and all peoples; however, they seem to be becoming more the norm with each passing decade.

Throughout the ages God has placed words in the mouths of His prophets. They spoke with all the authority of God Himself as they attempted to direct the people down the path that had been chosen for them by their Creator. Words are very powerful. Physicality is not necessary to bring down those in power. A few well-chosen words spoken to the right people at the right time can topple entire governments. Lies told in secret can explode into full public view overnight because of our addiction to social media.

With words God created. With words Satan deceived. With words God made promises. With words Christ taught. With words the enemies of Christ condemned Him to death. Things rise and fall with words. A corrupt heart wields words like a weapon. A pure heart uses them as a balm. Evil men say evil things and commit evil deeds. Righteous men speak the truth and bring life to all those who hear it. Nothing can silence words but death.

There are times when words are simply not enough. When sitting by the bedside of a loved one who is dying words seem to have no meaning, so you sit in silence. Comfort can lie in the things that are left unsaid. A tender touch or warm embrace trumps any words that could be spoken. There are times when we grope for the right words to say when words are not necessary. Our presence is more than enough and speaks volumes to the ones we are with. We struggle with what we feel are obligatory statements that we sense must be made to console or encourage, when the reality is that our eyes can express our deepest thoughts in a way that our tongue never could.

Judgment

People like to quote Matthew 7:1 regularly to keep people from pointing out that something they have said or done is wrong. "Don't judge or you too will be judged." Many times non-believers will throw that out there in an attempt to stop others in their tracks. I've seen some folks who have tattoos placed on their bodies stating, "Only God can judge me." So are Christians supposed to judge others? Scripture is pretty clear that we can judge fellow believers as a means of shining a light on an area that they may or may not be aware is in violation of God's word. I believe it would be more appropriate to call this 'loving correction' for all we do is to be done with the same mercy God has shown us. Galatians 6:1 provides our example: *"Brothers, if anyone is caught in any transgression, you who are spiritual should restore him in a spirit of gentleness. Keep watch on yourself, lest you too be tempted."* We should never use words as a weapon to make an example of a brother or sister in Christ. It is far better to approach them in private as a means of offering correction. If they resist, bring a witness and follow-up. The gospel of Matthew shows us in Jesus own words how to deal with such a situation in 18:15-20.

> "If your brother or sister sins, go and point out their fault, just between the two of you. If they listen to you, you have won them over. But if they will not listen, take one or two others along, so that 'every matter may be established by the testimony of two or three witnesses.' If they still refuse to listen, tell it to the church; and if they refuse to listen even to the church, treat them as you would a pagan or a tax collector."

We are not to judge non-believers, for their rejection of Christ has already pronounced them guilty. God alone shall judge those outside His hedge of protection.

Solomon's Insight Regarding 'Words'

Solomon's Proverbs were written down *"for gaining wisdom and instruction; for understanding **words** of insight"* (Proverbs 1:2). Proverbs tells us the following about the **words** of God written within its pages:

+ We are to accept them and store them up in our hearts.
+ Use Godly wisdom to avoid seductive words, thus avoiding temptation.
+ Take hold of God's words and keep His commands so that you will live.
+ We are not to forget them.
+ We are to turn our ears and pay attention to them.
+ We are to receive insight from them.

- They are just and true, with no falseness in them.
- We are instructed that prudent men hold their tongue and do not speak.

Other areas of scripture go on regarding words uttered by man and by God. One must understand that man's words can tend to be suspect; however, the words of God Almighty must never be doubted. Nothing we could ever say would mend a heart we have broken; but God heals. Although the consequences of our words may bring pain and suffering to those affected by us; God can bring restoration. We can stop the bleeding if we learn self-control. Learning to listen more and speak less is a helpful tool to avoid putting our foot in our mouth. We speak words without thinking and live with regret. God can change all that if we will only surrender our all to Him. Yes, even our speech. If the rudder steers the ship, let God take the helm. When will we realize we cannot make a go of this without God? Our words need to reflect a Godly influence in our lives if we claim to be a follower of Christ. Our words should heal and not hurt. God wants to teach us. His Holy Spirit wants to guide us into all truth. Once we understand the damage our words can do in mere seconds, perhaps we will respect their power and have less to say. We can learn nothing when we are doing the talking. It is only when we listen and truly hear that which God is trying to tell us that we can grow spiritually.

This has everything to do with our evangelistic efforts as well. The words we speak can draw people towards God or drive them away. Our words in this context are critical with eternal ramifications for those we are speaking to. We must seek the face of God before we open our mouths. We are Christ's representatives and we are to act like what we truly are. Remember, Jesus didn't scold or chastise unbelievers, but rather the believers who were supposed to know better. We are to speak words of consolation and compassion, healing and comfort, peace and hope to the lost souls around us. If they don't see Christ in us, why would they ever want listen to us. The Holy Spirit draws people in. Our witness is to be one filled with words of encouragement, forgiveness and life. How are we presenting God to others? We need to take a closer look at Jesus ministry to see what we are to do. That is one important reason why we must read His word. It should be our compulsion. We should want to read the Bible so that we can speak words that edify and not tear down. God knows what He's doing; let Him do a reconstruction in you so that you can best represent Him to a lost and dying world.

———◆———

"Words can be twisted into any shape. Promises can be made to lull the heart and seduce the soul. In the final analysis, words mean nothing. They are labels we give things …. The wisest man is the silent one. Examine his actions. Judge him by them."

Karen Marie Moning

CHAPTER 15

THE NEEDY AMONG US

"God helps those who help themselves"? [34]

Isn't that in the Bible? It sounds like something you'd find there, doesn't it? Although this statement is used frequently when referring to the poor, it can be found nowhere in scripture.

It implies that those who won't even lift a finger to help themselves don't deserve even God's help. There may be circumstances we are unaware of that have brought a person to their current lowly state. People speak those words as if they know all about it when they absolutely do not. It's curious to me that those who never even crack open a Bible are quick to pontificate using their extremely limited spiritual knowledge as a wedge to separate themselves from the "rabble" they are seeking to disassociate themselves from. They have neither sympathy, nor empathy for such people. David Livingstone (1813-1873), Scottish medical missionary to Africa, once said, "Sympathy is no substitute for action." We must do something, but what?

Terms Defined

The dictionary definition of 'poor' is to lack *sufficient* finances or possessions to live comfortably. 'Sufficient' is a relative word. I know people who appear to be quite comfortable, yet they are always clamoring for more because they believe they don't have enough. Those in the lowest economic stratum are those lacking the *necessities* of life. They are classified as 'needy'.

I happened to look up the statistics regarding those who were living below the federal poverty level. As of 2012 the new poverty level was determined to be $11,490 per individual. Census figures show that some 46 million Americans live below that level.[35] How did this happen? Sometimes individuals make poor life decisions that put them in a woeful state and sometimes life just happens. Sometimes you wind up in a financial place you never intended to be in due to a job layoff, bankruptcy or some sort of addiction; such as cigarettes, alcohol, drugs or gambling. It doesn't make that person a bum or lazy, it makes them one of the unfortunate people who have had bad things transpire in their lives. It happens to all sorts of people; people who had it coming to them, people who happened to be in the wrong place at the wrong time and yes, even people who would be classified as 'good' people. Society, generally speaking, shuns those less fortunate, assuming they must have deserved the condition they now find themselves in. At times, nothing could be further from the truth.

Having the financial rug pulled out from under you can create a feeling of panic and hopelessness. A person can tend to feel lost, out of sync or detached from the rest of the world. Despondency can immobilize a person, causing them to sit quietly for hours if not longer, mired in a sea of desperation. Those types of people find that they cannot help themselves. So if it were true that God helps those that help themselves, what on earth would become of folks like that?

To some, suicide seems like an attractive alternative to living in the circumstances they find themselves in. In 2010, it was reported in the New York Times Health section that more people lost their life by their own hand than in car accidents. There were 38,364 suicides to 33,687 auto accidents.[36] Despondency is a terrible thing. They see no hope, no way out, no light at the end of the tunnel. At times even Christians succumb to life's pressures and take their own life. No matter who we are or what trouble we're in, we must recognize our need for help and then simply ask for it. This is easy to say and not so easy to do. People are embarrassed by their situation or feel funny seeking assistance. When we ask God for help He may provide it in a wide variety of ways. God is there to help, but He forces Himself on no one.

We Must Ask

It's my belief that God would like to be very involved in all our lives; however, we have a free will so we can live as we choose with or without God having an active role in our lives. God is a gentleman. He doesn't bust down the door of our heart, but rather speaks to our heart by His Holy Spirit, gently wooing us to come to Him. We can do what we want with that; however, we must understand that God *doesn't* help those who do not seek His assistance. This applies equally to the needy, the wealthy and all economic strata in between. If God is no respecter of persons regarding His grace and His blessings, then why would it be any different when it comes to the assistance He provides? He doesn't dole out His blessings indiscriminately to all of creation, but to those who are part of His family. Assistance can come to the one who doesn't know God by way of others praying for them. They can certainly cry out to God for help, as can a loved one, friend or even a mere acquaintance that has been given a burden for that person. Help just doesn't happen. It must be sought. The homeless or poverty stricken or those hit with a severe catastrophic event need to seek God's assistance just like anyone else. Those who don't know God or how He operates may be expecting immediate relief from their circumstances if they pray and it may happen that way, but chances are it will not.

God Said He Would Save Me

One day a mighty storm hit a small town near the ocean. The rain fell, the winds roared and the waters rose. A man who refused to evacuate from his home was forced to climb onto his roof to stay dry. The water was up to the edge of his roof and the current was strong so the man decided to pray to God. He knew the Bible and therefore knew that God would save him. A little after he prayed a man came by in a row boat and asked if he could offer assistance. The man on the roof told him "No thank you, God is going to save me." Upon hearing his reply the man in the boat rowed off. The water continued to rise, inching closer to the man on the roof. Just then a rescue helicopter flew near and hovered over the man. The person in the helicopter offered to drop a life preserver and pull him up to safety, but the man on the roof again said "No thank you, God is going to save me." The water rose up to the man on the roof and the current carried him away. The man drown in the overwhelming flood waters. When he arrived in heaven he said to God "I asked You to save me. Your word promises to protect and save me from harm. Why didn't you save me?" God said "I sent you a man in a row boat and a Coast Guard Rescue helicopter, but you said 'No.' What were you expecting?"

It's important to watch for God's answers to prayer, for assistance may not always come in a way we expect. Those who are not accustomed to dealing with the spiritual realm give up hope rather easily much of the time. It's imperative that believers involved with helping the needy stay in regular touch with them to bolster them and reignite the hope that has been placed in their heart from our initial contact. God does not fail; *we* fail to rely on Him.

As a means of blaming someone for an individual's condition, some may ask 'Where is God?' It has to be someone's fault, doesn't it? Does it? Look at these verses in the Gospel of John:

"As he went along, he saw a man blind from birth. His disciples asked him, 'Rabbi, who sinned, this man or his parents, that he was born blind?' 'Neither this man nor his parents sinned,' said Jesus, 'but this happened so that the works of God might be displayed in him.'" (vv. 1-3)

No one did anything wrong to cause Hurricane Sandy to obliterate so many homes and take so many lives. No one's sin causes natural disasters of any kind to take place. It's my personal belief that God allowed these things to take place for His own purposes. To not believe that means there is something in this universe God created that He has no control over and *that* flies in the face of scripture and all it has to say about the power and might of God. I have no answers as to the 'why' of certain devastating events down through the ages, but God does if you choose to believe that.

Bad things happen to good people regardless of their economic status or moral character. Matthew 4:45 says, *"He (God) causes his sun to rise on the evil and the good, and sends rain on the righteous and the unrighteous."* Scripture is clear: *"all have sinned and fall short of the glory of God, and all are justified freely by his grace through the redemption that came by Christ Jesus."* (Romans 3:23b-24) Christ's death bought our freedom, but we must acknowledge our need of being redeemed and then receive the grace God so freely offers all men. This lone act bridges the gap that sin created between God and man.

A Matter of the Heart

Our heart's motivation is critical because God looks at the heart of a man and nothing else. *"But the LORD said to Samuel, "Do not look on his appearance or on the height of his stature, because I have rejected him. For* the LORD *sees not as man sees: man looks on the outward appearance, but* *the* LORD *looks on the heart.*" (1 Samuel 16:7) The Lord was talking to Samuel about Jesse's sons. God had picked one of the sons of Jesse to be the next King over Israel. Samuel thought surely one of Jesse's strong, young warrior sons would be God's choice; however, the Lord knew young David's heart. David was just a boy. He wasn't even brought before Samuel because he was out in the fields tending to the family flock of sheep. Jesse couldn't even imagine that David would be considered for such a lofty responsibility. This story regarding the calling of young David is a perfect example to us all that we must trust God in His assessment for He knows best. Although it may not have appeared to Samuel at the time, David was the proper choice for he was later referred to as '*a man after God's own heart*' (1 Samuel 13:14; Acts 13:22) and '*the* *apple of God's eye*' (Psalm 17:8).

It's possible that some efforts to help those in need are done solely to salve our conscience. It could also be because we felt an obligation and not a burden in our spirit. Perhaps we were coerced into helping. Helping others because of a burden God's Spirit has placed in our heart is called obedience. Constantly being open to assist those in need is a selfless act that extends the grace and mercy of God to those who may simply need a 'helping hand'. If we are unable to physically help them, we can support others who have such a burden. We can pray that God will provide assistance. We can donate money to an organization that helps others. Ask God to reveal avenues you can use to help others. Seek the wisdom of God.

As a side note, not all organizations are above board in all their dealings. As a means of example; my father sent donations out each month to a large number of organizations from animal shelters to medical assistance for the poor from other countries. I thought that was great! When I came home from Texas and lived with Dad for a while in the end of 2011, I became his Power of Attorney and began handling all financial and medical decisions for him. I sorted through his donations and checked with the Better Business Bureau regarding each one. One particular organization had a Founder/CEO who was being paid $702,000.00 per year in financial compensation. I immediately stopped sending them a donation check. *That* is precisely why we need to know who we are giving our hard earned money to.

Do We Really Want to be Like Christ?

I think sometimes we make it so difficult on ourselves. If we truly wish to emulate Christ then we will work on our relationship with God. It's the only way we can hear and understand the guidance He wants to give us. We have an advantage over non-believers in this regard. Millions of people who don't even pretend to know God do truly great things for the needy people of the world. Once those great deeds are done, what do they have to offer them? Once their home is reconstructed or their health is restored or their children are fed they may still eventually die in a sinful condition. Those who do not offer God's forgiveness are essentially helping dead people. That may sound strange to say, but if they live out their lives without the blood of Christ having washed away their sins, they will possibly live a good, honest, productive life only to die as unregenerate souls.

> *"If this is going to be a Christian nation that doesn't help the poor, either we have to pretend that Jesus was just as selfish as we are, or we've got to acknowledge that He commanded us to love the poor and serve the needy without condition and then admit that we just don't want to do it."*[37]

The gospel is without question good news, but it must be introduced in love and love is an action word. When we tell someone that we love them, is it passive? I sure hope not. Active love means you don't just speak the words, but show that individual not only that you love them but just how much. It seems to me that there are a variety of ways to help the poor and indigent. If everyone reached out to just one individual that was in need of some sort of assistance, we could make a real difference in this world. I'm afraid that we as Christians, as it states above, simply "don't want to do it". Perhaps we can't be bothered. We make excuses which we call reasons. Everything else seems more important to us. I'm exactly the same way, but I am trying to change. We can't help everyone all the time, but we can help those God puts us in contact with or at a time when we sense we are needed most.

There's no doubt that people need to be introduced to our Lord, but we can't make the introduction if they can't hear us. We have to live our faith before we can get them to listen to us. We must be careful not to fall into the trap of meeting a need solely for the purpose of getting them to listen. Oh, they may be listening, but there is a big difference between listening and hearing. We can listen to people all day long and not hear a thing.

When Hurricane Sandy devastated the Jersey Shore, along with Staten Island, New York City and Long Island, a whole lot of folks were in desperate need. They lost everything; their homes, contents and all. Most, but not all, escaped with their lives and the clothes on their backs as water came rushing down their streets. In the wake of such a tragedy, households opened their doors to near strangers and invited them to move in temporarily until they got themselves squared away. They stayed sometimes for months. That is true giving and a selfless act of love, mercy and grace. Many of those who opened up their homes had the ability to see themselves in that situation and reach out. Churches reached out.

It was a wonderful sight to see; God at work in the hearts and lives of people helping people.

As I have said, it seems to come out most when tragedy strikes. Sometimes lives are changed forever; sometimes for the better, sometimes for the worse. I know where God is in times such as these; right in the midst of it. But where is the Christian; hopefully on the front lines doing some good. Christians are human just like the rest of mankind. We get tired, bored, mad, embarrassed, frustrated, irritated and impatient. If you cut us we bleed just like anyone else. It's regrettable that non-believers only see us as rigid, legalistic, pompous airbags who talk a good talk but don't back it up with actions. Every facet of mankind has its slackers and phonies and Christianity isn't excluded. Perhaps our good deeds go unnoticed because we do it unto God and not unto men? We don't necessarily broadcast our actions or our good deeds, but rather do what we do without fanfare. We desire that all glory go where it belongs, to God and God alone. When we slip up and act inappropriately it seems as though the whole entire world is watching with no place for us to hide. No slack is given and no pardon is forthcoming. That's alright. As Christians we know that God knows all about it, understands and His pardon is for the asking. I would rather know I am forgiven by God than by man any day of the week.

———⊶◎⊷———

"The most eloquent prayer is the prayer through hands that heal and bless."

Billy Graham

CHAPTER 16

FORGIVENESS

"Then Peter came to Jesus and asked, 'Lord, how many times shall I forgive my brother when he sins against me? Up to seven times?' Jesus answered, 'I tell you, not seven times, but seventy-seven times.'" (Matthew 18:21-22)

"To be a Christian means to forgive the inexcusable because God has forgiven the inexcusable in you." - C.S. Lewis

"Forgiveness is not an occasional act, it is a constant attitude." - Martin Luther King Jr.

"Forgiveness is not about forgetting. It is about letting go of another person's throat." - Wm. Paul Young

"The willingness to forgive is a sign of spiritual and emotional maturity. It is one of the great virtues to which we all should aspire. - Gordon B. Hinckley

"Forgiveness is an act of the will, and the will can function regardless of the temperature of the heart." - Corrie ten Boom

As Christians we are to forgive those who treat us poorly. In Matthew 5:23-24, Jesus tells His listeners if someone has something against us, we are to leave our gift at the altar and go make things right with that person. We are not to expect them to come to us; we are to be proactive. Go to them and be reconciled, than offer your gift.

I placed the quotations at the beginning of the chapter as a precursor or introduction to the topic of forgiveness. Let's take a quick look at each of them.

When Jesus tells Peter to forgive 70 x 7 times, this is symbolic of an infinite number of times. How many times does God forgive the same dumb things that we do repeatedly? God will forgive us an infinite number of times as long as we seek forgiveness. We are told that God casts our sins into the *"depths of the sea"* (Micah 7:18-19). In Psalm 103:12 it tells us: *"As far as the east is from the west, so far has he removed our transgressions from us."*

CS Lewis, noted Christian author and speaker, points out that when we forgive someone we are not doing such a great thing for we are doing no more for another than God Himself did for us. It's true. Scripture says in Ephesians 4:32 to forgive just as in Christ God forgave us. There are no instances that we are not to forgive.

Martin Luther King, Jr. alerts us that forgiveness is to be a continuous attitude and not a hit and run endeavor. We aren't to pick and choose whom we will forgive, but rather forgive others as we have been forgiven. Paul Young illustrates forgiveness in a rather vivid way, giving us the mental picture of letting go of the throat of the one we are at odds with. Gordon Hinckley reveals to us that our willingness to forgive others is a sign of maturity; both spiritual and emotional. If more people were willing to forgive, this world would undoubtedly be a much more pleasant place to live. Corrie Ten Boom, Christian holocaust survivor, tells us that our forgiveness has nothing to do with how we feel about a person or situation.

There should be no delay in offering forgiveness; however, trust is another story. The person forgiven must understand that he must build up his questionable integrity over time before the offended party will trust him again. That's where the whole forgetting issue comes into play. I may readily forgive someone, but I tend to remember the offense so it doesn't happen to me again. I don't hold it against the person, nor do I resent them; I simply remember it in the deeper recesses of my mind so as not to get burned again.

Resentment

There are times in every person's life when their anger gets the better of them. Like water coming to a rolling boil, they allow an event or an individual to cause them to become so hot under the collar that it gives birth to resentment. A seed of bitterness will wreak havoc on the heart and spirit of even the strongest Christian. Non-believers have no hope against such an adversary for they have no reinforcements to call on from within themselves. Bitterness when allowed to come to full bloom will not harm the object of your disdain; it will only harm you. The late Nelson Mandela has something to say regarding resentment that is very profound in its simplicity. He says, *"Resentment is like drinking poison and then hoping it will kill your enemies."* There isn't much you can add to that.

God's Forgiveness

Forgiveness is one of the cornerstones of the Christian faith. Would we even know we were sinners separated from God in need of forgiveness if we weren't told? It seems very likely we wouldn't. It's said that we are born with an inherent sense of right and wrong. We have proven that with the free will God provides us we have a distinct proclivity towards doing the wrong thing.

If man was capable of doing such good why was it necessary for Noah to build an ark? It took Noah and his sons 120 years to construct the ark; time enough for mankind to repent and turn to God. Once completed, God instructed Noah to place his family and two of each animal created into the ark. Once the door was shut, God brought 40 days and nights of rain flooding the earth. As a result, all the unrepentant were destroyed. Those in the ark were the only survivors.

If man were good, why were annual sin sacrifices necessary to cleanse the Jewish men of their sins? If man were good, why did Jesus have to die? I submit to you that man is inherently evil at his core without God, for even when he does good it typically has some ulterior motive attached.

To receive forgiveness from God, we must admit our sins and receive the redemption that God freely offers in the person of His Son Jesus Christ. As a result of our conversion, God's Holy Spirit begins to bring about changes in us that cause us to live for God and others rather than ourselves. God offers His forgiveness for all the sinning we had done up to the point of our conversion and continues to forgive us of the sins we commit afterwards if we admit our need of forgiveness and make the 180 degree turn that is required.

> *"If we confess our sins, he is faithful and just and will forgive us our sins and purify us from all unrighteousness."*
> (1 John 1:9)

On man's best day his most gracious and kind act would do nothing to earn his place in heaven. There is nothing we can do to earn forgiveness accept receive what Christ did for us on Calvary's cross. We must become a new creature through spiritual rebirth. It's then that our sins are forgiven. The wonderful thing about past sins is they're never held against us again. When we continue living in sin after forgiveness has been given to us, we trample God's grace under foot. God's forgiveness should reveal to us how we are to treat those who offend us, but we are lazy regarding Biblical instruction many times and are not as close to our Heavenly Father as we could and should be. We need to allow our character to be molded into one that resembles that of Christ. We are to be instruments of peace, encouragement, edification, forgiveness and hope. Nothing else is acceptable. We must give our lives away. We must surrender our will to God. What we want in this life is far inferior to what God has in store for His children. That's why it's so important to involve God in all our important, life changing decisions.

Trampling On God's Grace

We can't allow ourselves to fall into the trap of withholding God's grace from those around us we don't care for. While we aren't God, we are His representatives in this world and the only examples this world has to go by regarding what God is like. We must take our walk with God seriously. We need to feed our spirit man, thus keeping our faith strong. There are so many poor examples of Christians in the world today. They bludgeon brothers and sisters instead of restore them. They bash certain sectors of humanity feeling they are doing God's work. Nowhere in scripture does it tell us to be judge and jury over the non-believer. That's God's job. If God treated us the way we treat others we wouldn't like that one bit. God forgives and expects His children, who *have* been forgiven, to alter their wrong behavior instead of becoming a lightning rod for controversy. The idea is that we draw attention to our Heavenly Father in a positive way, not in a contentious, argumentative way. We have caused many unnecessary obstacles to rise up around us because of our unwillingness to forgive. Emulating Christ is something we should want to do. As His ambassadors it's our responsibility to understand what is required of us in the name of the Lord and diligently strive to achieve those characteristics necessary to show people their need of placing faith in Almighty God. Without forgiveness our mission is idling in neutral. Without forgiveness we have missed the point. It seemed so clear when *we* received forgiveness. Now our vision has become blurred.

The Jonah Factor

> "The word of the LORD came to Jonah son of Amittai: 'Go to the great city of Nineveh and preach against it, because its wickedness has come up before me.' But Jonah ran away from the LORD and headed for Tarshish." (Jonah 1:1-3a)

> "But to Jonah this seemed very wrong, and he became angry. He prayed to the Lord, 'Isn't this what I said, Lord, when I was still at home? That is what I tried to forestall by fleeing to Tarshish. I knew that you are a gracious and compassionate God, slow to anger and abounding in love, a God who relents from sending calamity. Now, Lord, take away my life, for it is better for me to die than to live.' But the Lord replied, 'Is it right for you to be angry?'" (Jonah 4:1-4)

The point of this story in scripture is that we may not always like what God asks us to do, such as forgiving a person we are greatly at odds with, but God is running the show and He did not balk when it came to forgiving us. The Lord does what He chooses without seeking permission for there is no one higher than God. We have no right to complain or disagree with God, for we do not know His purposes.

Misplaced Anger

God does, however, allow us to vent our frustrations with what we may perceive as injustice. If we jump over to the final chapters of the Book of Job, we may understand a little better why our anger and frustration is misplaced. In Job 38-39 God asks a litany of questions to which Job has no answer. God establishes the fact that He alone knows all things and not man.

> *"Then Job answered the* LORD: *'I am unworthy—how can I reply to you? I put my hand over my mouth. I spoke once, but I have no answer— twice, but I will say no more.' Then the* LORD *spoke to Job out of the storm: 'Brace yourself like a man; I will question you, and you shall answer me.'"* (Job 40:3-7)

In all that the Lord says to Job, He reveals the feebleness of Job's thoughts and abilities. Job ultimately repents before God for speaking *"of things I did not understand, things too wonderful for me to know"*. His surrender to God resulted in Job repenting in dust and ashes, which was customary of those at that time who were remorseful of sins committed against Jehovah God. Under the dispensation of grace we are no longer required to do such a thing as a means of showing our remorse; however, our behavior should be altered for the future. We can never know the mind of God so it behooves us to simply obey Him and know that His purposes are much higher than we could ever comprehend. Forgiveness is to be given quickly and readily without personal emotions entering into our decision. We must take into consideration what state *we* would be in if God had decided to arbitrarily withdraw His forgiveness from us. He doesn't and never will, therefore neither should we.

"Forgiveness is the final form of love."
Reinhold Niebuhr

CHAPTER 17

Jesus & C.S. Lewis

A Snapshot Portrait

He was and is the most fascinating character to ever walk the face of the earth. Who was Jesus of Nazareth? Christianity teaches that He was born on this earth by the hand of God. As we saw in earlier chapters, not everyone believes that.

According to the New Testament in the Bible, a young virgin named Mary was chosen by God to bear a miraculously conceived child. Mary was found to be with child just as an Angel had proclaimed to her as written in Luke 1:26-38.

When she was great with child Mary and her husband Joseph went to Bethlehem to take part in a census ordered by Caesar Augustus. If you think you have it rough, consider walking an estimated 4-5 days over rough terrain with your very pregnant wife riding sidesaddle on a beast of burden. This was no picnic, yet it was another piece in a puzzle called God's plan for the salvation of mankind.

An angel of God proclaimed the Messiah's arrival to the shepherds watching their flocks by night and 3 Wise Men or Magi saw "His star when it rose" in the night sky (Matthew 2:2b) and were going to worship Him.

King Herod, the Roman appointed king of the Jews, was less than pleased when he found out about this king of the Jews being born. Any opposition to his rule would not be tolerated, even if it were a mere infant. Herod called for the Magi and asked them to report back to him where the child lay so that the King could go and worship Him as well. After having seen the child, an angel warned the Magi to take another route home, for God knew the evil intent in Herod's heart. Jesus had a mission from the Father and nothing was going to derail the plan God had set in motion.

As Jesus grew He was raised, as any other Jewish boy would be, under the tutelage of His mother Mary until he was 13. At that point in his life, Jesus would no longer be taught by His mother but by His earthly father, Joseph. Two verses in the gospels reveal to us the following about Joseph's trade. In Matthew 13:55, the people in the synagogue that heard Jesus speak with wisdom were stunned asking, "Isn't this the carpenter's son?" This tells us that Joseph was recognized by the townspeople as one who worked with wood. Mark's rendition of the same event has the crowd abuzz saying amongst themselves "Isn't this the carpenter?" Though not critically important, one can assume based on these two verses in scripture that Joseph was a carpenter and as is the Jewish tradition, the father teaches his son the same trade he practices; therefore Jesus was also a carpenter.

In Luke 2:39-52, we read about Joseph and Mary going to Jerusalem for the Festival of the Passover, which took place annually. After the Festival was over, they started for home. Once they had gotten a considerable distance into their journey they noticed that Jesus wasn't with them.

Today, when kidnappings take place regularly, parents have learned to have an eagle eye when it comes to the whereabouts of their children. How could Mary and Joseph lose track of Jesus? Luke's account tells us in verse 44 that it wasn't just Mary, Joseph and Jesus making this trip; it was a caravan with relatives and friends. So it is not so crazy to think that their son was with the other children in the caravan. Today they would have done a head count, back then it wasn't necessary. If Jesus wasn't with the caravan, just exactly where was He? As it turns out, He was in the temple listening to the teachers and asking them questions. All who engaged him in conversation saw Jesus as an extraordinary young man due to the wisdom He regularly displayed.

As a side note, notice that though Jesus was God's Son, albeit only 12 years old at the time, He *listened* and *asked questions* of the teachers in the temple. By doing this He showed them respect. Christians today could take a lesson from this account. You learn nothing new by speaking. It's only by listening intently to others that you can learn anything; especially when it comes to things worth knowing, such as the things of God.

When Jesus reached 30 years of age, John the Baptist baptized Him in the river Jordan. It was at that precise moment the heavens opened and God's spirit descended on Jesus like a dove. God uttered the words "This is my Son, in whom I am well pleased." Luke's accounting of this event gives us a confirmation of Jesus' divinity. It was time for His ministry to begin. After He was baptized, the Holy Spirit immediately took Jesus into the wilderness where Satan tempted him. This period of testing lasted 40 days and nights after which angels tended to His needs.

Luke 4:14-28 tells of the time Jesus spoke in His hometown synagogue. He ruffled feathers in the synagogue by announcing for all to hear that he was the fulfillment of the Isaiah's prophecy regarding the coming Messiah. They wanted to run him out of town; however, He simply walked through the angry mob untouched and went on His way. The will of God could not be stopped or altered.

His ministry lasted 3 years. During that time Jesus taught of His Father, healed the sick and even raised dead men back to life. The Jewish religious leaders saw Jesus as a threat to the established laws and commands handed down from God by Moses and marked Him for death.

They finally got their wish as they had Jesus brought before Pontius Pilate, the Roman prefect for the province of Judea, as a subversive. They wished for Him to be crucified, which was the way the Romans put criminals to death. It was a slow, torturous death showing us that the Jewish leaders wanted Jesus to suffer for what He had been doing. Christ was murdered for differing ideologically with the Jewish religious leaders of His day; in their minds a just punishment for a alleged heretic. Jesus would allow Himself to be whipped with a scourge, which was a multi-talon whip covered with pieces of jagged bone, metal and beads of lead. This item was meant to inflict agony beyond description as it dug into the flesh of its victim and tore chunks of meat from their body. Jesus was disrespected, disgraced and treated with disgust by the Roman soldiers who didn't know any better. To them He was nothing more than today's target for amusement. But the Jewish leaders should have known who this man truly was. Their own pride and arrogance blinded them from seeing the true nature of this man.

Christianity shows unequivocally through scripture that Jesus Christ was not merely a moral teacher or prophet as some say. He was the Son of the one true and living God as revealed in scripture. His death, burial and bodily resurrection ignited the ember of faith that was still glowing within the hearts of His seemingly abandoned disciples. When Christ appeared to them after He had arisen it fanned the flame into a blaze of boldness that gave birth to the church throughout Asia Minor and beyond. We believe today because Jesus Christ came, ministered to the masses, died and rose again to new life. His blood sacrifice provided payment for the sins of all who would receive it; forgiveness was and is offered to all, yet it must be accepted, as any gift would be and applied to our life.

Jesus is the key

All the people who claim there is no proof that God exists equally demand proof that Jesus was the Son of God. God does not and will not do miraculous things to provide proof to the unbeliever. That would be tantamount to casting pearls before swine (Matthew 7:6). Since belief in God and Jesus Christ as the Son of God requires faith, no amount of proof would ever convince anyone of His existence. John 20:24-29 tells about Thomas who doubted that Jesus had come back from the dead. He said *"Unless I see the nail marks in his hands and put my finger where the nails were, and put my hand into his side, I will not believe."* Well he saw them and he felt them and dropped to his needs to worship the risen Lord. Jesus subsequently declares in verse 29, *"Because you have seen me, you have believed; blessed are those who have not seen and yet have believed."* That, my friends, is you and I if we have placed our trust in Jesus Christ to forgive us of all our sins. We are blessed in the eyes of God.

Skeptics will always have one more question. They will find the one thing you couldn't answer and hang their hat of disbelief on that. Even today, if Jesus Himself appeared before *some* people, they would still want proof of His identity. It was no different than the religious leaders of Jesus day. He did miracle after miracle and instead of allowing these events to convince them that He was the Messiah prophesied in the scriptures, they became irate that He was breaking the Mosaic Law by, for example, healing someone on the Sabbath (Mark 3:1-6). Plotting to kill Christ was all part of God's plan for He knew the Jewish religious leaders would reject Jesus as the Christ. None of this was a shock to God; He foresaw it all. It was the one way to introduce His grace, mercy and forgiveness to the non-Jew.

It's interesting and curious that while Muslims, Jews and Christians all believe in the same God, they all differ in their interpretation and ultimate acceptance of Jesus as the savior of mankind. All other religions put the onus on the individual to live a certain lifestyle according to standards set by someone other than God. Jesus either didn't exist at all or is a mere mortal who is no different than any other prophet or teacher throughout history. How tragic to miss the importance of this man.

CS Lewis weighs in

Clive Staples Lewis (1898-1963) was a British novelist and essayist who is best known to us as C.S. Lewis. Lewis was born in Belfast, Ireland. While at Oxford in the 1920s, Lewis moved from being an atheist to a committed Christian. His most popular Christian works are The Screwtape Letters (1942), relating the advice given by a senior devil, Screwtape, to his subordinate, Wormwood, in luring a human subject away from salvation; Mere Christianity (1952, but originally a series of radio talks begun in 1941); and his spiritual autobiography Surprised by Joy. He also wrote a science-fiction trilogy (1938–45) and the seven children's books known as the Chronicles of Narnia (1950–6), which incorporate Christian themes allegorically. The death of his wife, Joy Davidson, evoked the searching record of his grief, A Grief Observed (first published under the name N. W. Clerk).

Why have I mentioned Mr. Lewis in this book? Because Lewis was a champion of Christianity in that he articulately voiced his belief in God through stark illustrations. One of his most famous is the following:

> "I am trying here to prevent anyone saying the really foolish thing that people often say about Him: I'm ready to accept Jesus as a great moral teacher, but I don't accept his claim to be God. That is the one thing we must not say. A man who was merely a man and said the sort of things Jesus said

would not be a great moral teacher. He would either be a lunatic — on the level with the man who says he is a poached egg — or else he would be the Devil of Hell. You must make your choice. Either this man was, and is, the Son of God, or else a madman or something worse. You can shut him up for a fool, you can spit at him and kill him as a demon or you can fall at his feet and call him Lord and God, but let us not come with any patronizing nonsense about his being a great human teacher. He has not left that open to us. He did not intend to. … Now it seems to me obvious that He was neither a lunatic nor a fiend: and consequently, however strange or terrifying or unlikely it may seem, I have to accept the view that He was and is God."[38]

Lewis, in <u>Mere Christianity</u>, called this the great Trilemma: "Christ either deceived mankind by conscious fraud, or He was Himself deluded and self-deceived, or He was Divine. There is no getting out of this trilemma. It is inexorable." We may see Christ any way we would like, but the fact remains that He lived on this earth over 2000 years ago and has to be dealt with.

Zeal vs. Apathy

When C.S. Lewis spoke, he did so from a vast treasure trove of knowledge acquired through study, prayer, perseverance & discipline. Modern day believers too often want to speak before we know what to say. We struggle with two things: being overzealous and being apathetic. Zeal is a wonderful thing. It speaks of boldness in the face of opposition; however, it can be overdone, looking like arrogance to some. Being overzealous to the point of offending others in the name of the gospel is a profoundly wrong way to go about evangelizing. The world doesn't understand God and it surely doesn't understand Christians. We say one thing and do another, seeming quite hypocritical as we display a 'do-what-I-say, not-what-I-do' type of unspoken attitude. The world already thinks ill of us because we represent what they see as structured restriction. An approach that is less 'in your face' and more loving is in order. Not just saying words that ring hollow in the face of an unmet need, but rather actions that actually meet that need. Jesus never went about lambasting every sinful person He laid eyes on.

As I stated earlier, He tore into the religious leaders, not those who had yet to be forgiven. Christians are God's appointed representatives. If we are using Christ as our example of how to act and react in this lost and dying world, then where in scripture did He say or do any of the harsh, insensitive, judgmental things we have done in His name? We are at times pathetic shadows of what we can be because we allow our own egos to get in the way of what God is trying to do through us. Is it any wonder the world turns their back on God and thinks of us as they do?

Another thing we must get through our heads is that they are unfamiliar with our Christian jargon. Words like salvation, sanctification or repentance mean nothing to the unsaved. We must focus on God's leading and speak in a language they can understand. The unspoken language of love, mercy and compassion hope say far more to an individual than our actual words ever could. It gives people hope.

The damage is not irreparable, but that is only because of God. We can climb from the ashes of our own shortcomings and do great and wonderful things in the name of Jesus, but we have to remember that *He* must increase and *we* must decrease (John 3:30). He *must!* We cannot do anything of any lasting eternal value without Christ. If we show this world Christ in a real and profound way and they still turn their backs, then we have done all we can do.

Why Are We Failing?

Could it be that the wait for Christ's return has dulled our senses or perhaps we have developed an attitude that we are somehow deserving of eternity with God while others are not? We must always recognize that eternity hangs in the balance for the lost souls of this world. We must temper zeal with love. We must meet needs rather than grow weary of doing good (Galatians 6:9). We send mixed messages to a non-believing world as we become walking, talking contradictions. Actions definitely and without question speak much louder than words ever could. We can shout the gospel from a rooftop and it will never make as much of an impact as giving someone a blanket when they are cold or a warm meal when they are hungry. We must *be* Christ to this dying world. It isn't easy, but anything worthwhile typically isn't. We don't have to do it all and we don't have to be in control. God is in control and we are to be the vessels; the conduits He has chosen to use in spite of ourselves. God overlooks our flaws and shortcomings, just as we are to do the same with those around, both believers and non- believers.

I've mentioned the terrible storm that ripped through our area in October 2012 with devastation and loss of life the result. We are still having difficulty wrapping our collective minds around the fact that some buildings that have been iconic in nature and stood for years are no longer standing. People died. It doesn't seem to compute. Well, in a way that's what we need to think about when we think about lost souls; we may be the only Jesus they ever see in this life. The storm we can prepare for; brace ourselves, hunker down and endure it, but just by speaking up or better still acting on Jesus' behalf we may keep some folks from a fiery eternity. It's up to us to reach out. God hasn't ordered the final trumpet to be blown yet. There is time until God stops the clock. Be mindful of the opportunities to speak out for God. Remember, God doesn't need us, but rather has chosen to use us and the world needs the Lord.

"Being a Christian is more than just an instantaneous conversion - it is a daily process whereby you grow to be more and more like Christ."

Billy Graham

CHAPTER 18

ARE CHRISTIANS THE PROBLEM?

"Do not merely listen to the word, and so deceive yourselves. Do what it says. Anyone who listens to the word but does not do what it says is like someone who looks at his face in a mirror and, after looking at himself, goes away and immediately forgets what he looks like." (James 1:22-24)

Throughout this book I have touched on topics I felt were relevant to us as Christians. There were many statements and phrases that I repeated often for emphasis. Are we really the main problem when it comes to the spreading of our belief system? Are we a people who listen to the Word of God without doing what it says? Are we looking in a mirror and seeing nothing? Only we as individuals can answer that. How do we represent our Lord? Is it contrary to how Christ lived when He walked the earth? In our haste to *do* something, do we enter the fray ill prepared? How many times has our zeal or boldness caused us embarrassment or shame? Enthusiasm regarding our newfound beliefs is a wonderful and exciting thing to experience; however, we mustn't lead with zeal, but rather with the spirit. Even a new believer, if humble enough to ask the Lord to give him words to say, can be a powerful representative of God. It's the believer, new or seasoned, who thinks of himself and his Biblical knowledge more highly then he ought that gives Christianity a bad name. Always remember what I have been saying throughout this book; God doesn't *need* us to propagate the gospel, He has *chosen to use* us. Like anything else in life, whether it is athletics or a company job, we must be trained to perform at peak efficiency. We must learn to use spiritual discernment when it comes to obtaining direction and understanding from God.

Be Quiet & Listen

> *"My dear brothers and sisters, take note of this: Everyone should be quick to listen, slow to speak ..."* (James 1:19a)

Sometimes we as Christians shoot our mouths off in circumstances where we should be silent. That may be regarding a witnessing endeavor or just a casual conversation. We mistakenly believe that we have something vital to say, yet at times only come off sounding either arrogant, ignorant ... or both. We cannot learn anything if we are talking. We must learn to control our tongue and listen to those that are speaking to us. No matter who they are or what they believe, listening to those around us helps us understand where they're coming from. We really need to *hear* others though. I must confess that there have been times when I was so busy thinking about what I was going to say next that I had no idea what the person speaking to me was saying. That smacks of conceit in a way, because we are assuming that what we have to say is superior to whatever anyone else is saying. We have to get over that.

We also don't need to get ourselves into arguments or needless debates. It's not our mission to engage others in senseless conversations that produce nothing worth remembering. Non-believers love word play. They ask nonsensical questions almost in a mocking tone as a means of stymieing us. Heaven or hell issues are paramount, nothing more. You cannot force anyone to believe in God or accept Christ any more than you can teach a pig to fly. They must choose for themselves in whom they will believe. We are commissioned to plant, water and at times harvest seeds. If we do our part with a humble, obedient spirit God shall bring the increase. Since the Christian belief system is based on faith alone, we are to lay it out for people as so led by God's Spirit. The rest is up to the hearer.

The Same But Different

Each one of us has our own unique personalities and characteristics; yet we are all sinners in God's eyes up until we accept the redemptive work Christ performed on Calvary's cross. Once a person receives forgiveness for their sins, they enter into a right relationship with God. It isn't Nirvana or Shangri-La. Christians still have an abundance of problems to deal with. We all still have to earn a living. We still have bills to pay. We still get sick. We still eventually die, just like anyone else. The difference is in how we handle our problems. The difference is in the peace we have during trying situations. Do we, as Christians, lose our temper? Sure. Do we slip and drop an F-Bomb from time to time? Uh-huh. Do we fret and worry about things we can do nothing about? Yes, sir. But we are learning to live a better life where the problems don't go away, but the way we handle them becomes different. Naturally, an unbelieving world driven by scandals and the latest big story will always announce in big bold type that a 'born-again' Christian has had an affair or fallen back into an addictive habit. I believe God watches in great disappointment at times for how we botch up His message, but the thing God gives us that the world never will is grace, mercy, forgiveness and another opportunity to get it right. Regardless of whether we try to force feed the gospel message down people's throats or practice friendship evangelism, it is ultimately the non-believers choice. Sure, a forceful approach can be a turn off, but God's word doesn't return void (Isaiah 55:11).

The reason I often say that we must surrender to God is because to think we can do anything for the kingdom without the wisdom, guidance and direction of God's Holy Spirit is wrong thinking. We are fooling ourselves to think we can go forward for the kingdom on our own, armed only with our meager understanding of scripture. God has offered to equip us, but we bellow, objecting that we *"have no time"* or *"time is running out; souls are dying without Christ every day."* Remember, to God time is nothing. We place far too great an importance on the passing of time. We are certainly not to sit idly by doing nothing, but rather wait patiently for the hand of God to move on our behalf. Read scripture, pray for wisdom, guidance and discernment; feed your spirit through the written word, the spoken word and through the lyrics of songs. As we go about our day, we should be ever mindful of those around us who are lost. God's desire is to see none of them perish. We are to go about our business as believers prayerfully. God knows what He's doing. He isn't going to forget anything nor are we going to gain anything by becoming frustrated with delays. It's called 'resting' in God. The closer we get to Him, the more at ease we will become. The Holy Spirit will work in us to change the way we look at circumstances and how we handle ourselves within them, but it doesn't happen unless we allow Him to do His work in us.

All In God's Time

We don't have to all become what the world calls 'bible thumpers'. As we trust in and rely upon our God to provide for and sustain us in all areas of our lives, we will begin to know Him better. We will relax in the spirit and realize that God's plan is being worked out all around us all the time. People we meet each day are there for a purpose. Perhaps they are there to challenge our faith; perhaps to encourage us. As we understand that each event that takes place is designed and orchestrated by our Heavenly Father we come to understand that He really is in control of all things and will take good care of us as long as we trust Him to do so. This all helps us reach out to those around us with a peaceful spirit. We have no reason to panic or race ahead of God as if He were moving too slowly.

Our lives are to be a reflection of His love and mercy. God is the judge, not us. Yes, we are allowed to be fruit inspectors, discerning whether a believer is truly who he is portraying himself to be. A tree not cared for properly will either bare a scarce amount of fruit or no fruit at all. A phony Christian is easy to spot for that very reason; no fruit.

We are allowed to rebuke a brother or sister for their words or actions, but only when we have solid scripture to back us up. We must also do it in love with a spirit of humility. We are not supposed to lambast those who live in a non-believing world, but rather do as God did for us; relate in some small way to them and be as *genuinely consistent* as possible as we strive to exemplify the love, mercy and grace of God. There may be some folks who require a heavy hand spiritually speaking, but that is for God to decide and not us.

Too many times our decisions are tainted by prejudice and pre-judgment. There is none of that from God. He views us all the same; from the vilest death row criminal, to the prostitute on the street, to the corporate man in the suit and tie or the homemaker with four children. It makes no difference to God and it shouldn't to us either. We must learn to see all people the way God sees them. I am as guilty as the next person regarding this issue. We must determine to see each unsaved individual as if they were walking over a fiery abyss on a tight rope. Only Christ can bridge that abyss. That is what the gospel is all about; that is the good news we have to share.

Let the Spirit Bring Conviction

Are we the problem? Are we the reason people are turning away from God? Maybe in some small part; but to some people, someone else will always be the problem; never them. I can tell you one way that isn't going to get positive results. Online just this morning I spied a picture on Google Images of a Church message board out front that said the following: "God saw you do that." Please allow me to vent; on what planet do those people think that will be effective? First of all, God sees everything, so that isn't much of a revelation. To the unbeliever it is just another clanging cymbal. Do we want to guilt people into salvation or do we want to speak words of comfort, peace and forgiveness. I know God is a God of wrath and judgment, but that is for the end of time and not right now.

I remember once many years ago at the alter up front after one of those End Times movies that our church was showing, a teenage boy came up to me for salvation. He said he was a member of the local Methodist church. "What can I pray with you about", I asked. His answer: "I don't want to go to hell." Now is that really our mission? Really? Get people into heaven whatever way we can. Wow. Yeah, let's scare the hell out of everyone. That'll work. What we are supposed to do is not scare them, but rather speak peace to them. Share the forgiveness that is readily available. Conviction comes from the Holy Spirit. We shouldn't manufacture it for that ends up being pure guilt and nothing else. Conviction is a deep regret that goes way beyond mere human guilt feelings. God's Spirit brings it on as He reveals to the seeker the true condition of their heart.

No Compromise

In all that I have said within the pages of this book, I want to emphasize that there is no room for compromising the message of Christ crucified, for therein lies the crux of our faith. In our efforts to relate to others or even tolerate others we are never to white wash our message. We didn't write the message we're only delivering it.

Christians are said to be intolerant of those who don't agree with their beliefs. I beg to differ. While there are exceptions to every rule, it is my belief that Christians tolerate opposition reasonably well. It's those who fear us that are the most intolerant. Oh, they would never admit their fear, but how else could you explain their hateful and loathsome attitude towards us. Every group has its bad apples, no question about it; but should an entire religious group be attacked just because a small fraction of the general population doesn't see eye to eye with their beliefs. It must be Jesus; there's just something about that name.

The phrase 'genuine consistency' has been used frequently throughout this book. I see it as the common thread that ties everything together. Unless you are *consistently genuine* in your faith you will just be more white noise to those around you.

It's my sincere hope that this book has helped the reader understand what we may be doing to turn off non-believers. Sprinkled throughout has been my opinion with a heavy dose of scripture backing. Once we take the time to truly see Jesus Christ for who He is rather than who we are told He is and begin to emulate Him as portrayed in scripture, I believe we will live a much more productive life for the Kingdom of God. You can be sure that there will always be those who shun God and hate us, but at least we will know why and can learn to shrug it off. It's important to always remember that the world is not rejecting us they are rejecting Almighty God. We are the messengers God is the message giver. I leave you with this final question: What message are you sending to those around you about your beliefs and your God?

———◦———

"Humility is not thinking less of yourself, it's thinking of yourself less."
C. S. Lewis

ENDNOTES

[1] http://www.christianpost.com/news/how-do-unchurched-americans-view-christianity

[2] Quote by Austin Cline; Cline was a Regional Director for the Council for Secular Humanism and a former Publicity Coordinator for the Campus Free-Thought Alliance. Austin has also lectured on religion, religious violence, science, and skepticism.

[3] *Matthew*; Craig S. Keener; The IVP New Testament Commentary Series; IVP Academic; 1997. Craig S. Keener is a professor of the New Testament at Asbury Theological Seminary, Wilmore, Kentucky.

[4] http://www.religioustolerance.org/bugliosi01.htm; Victor Bugliosi; Why Do I Doubt Both the Atheists and the Theists?

[5] The story that is widely circulated is that the phrase was first spoken by the English evangelical preacher and martyr, John Bradford (circa 1510–1555). He is said to have uttered the variant of the expression - "There but for the grace of God, goes John Bradford", when seeing criminals being led to the scaffold.

[6] *Magnum Force*; Warner Bros.; 1973.

[7] Article by 'Elaine' on www.gaychurch.org web site.

[8] *The law lags, God blesses same-sex unions*; Michael Riley; Asbury Park Press; July 13, 2013.

[9] http://www.biography.com/people/david-koresh

[10] http://www.biography.com/people/jim-jones

[11] http://www.don-lindsay-archive.org/scientology/start.a.religion.html

[12] "Buddhism." International Encyclopedia of the Social Sciences. 1968. *Encyclopedia.com*.

[13] http://www.encyclopedia.com/topic/Hinduism.aspx

[14] Information taken from http://www.differencebetween.net/miscellaneous/difference-between-christianity-and-hinduism/

[15] www.oxforddictionaries.com/islam

[16] http://www.discoveringislam.org/islam_vs_christianity.htm

[17] Exodus 20:3; 20:23; 34:14; Deuteronomy 5:7; 6:14; 2 Kings 17:35; Psalm 81:9; Isaiah 42:8; Jeremiah 25:6; Hosea 13:4.

[18] Bowker, John. "Sin." The Concise Oxford Dictionary of World Religions. 1997. *Encyclopedia.com*. (October 25, 2012). http://www.encyclopedia.com/doc/1O101-Sin.html

[19] Bowker, John. "Sin." The Concise Oxford Dictionary of World Religions. 1997. *Encyclopedia.com*. (October 25, 2012). http://www.encyclopedia.com/doc/1O101-Sin.html

[20] Bowker, John. "Sin." The Concise Oxford Dictionary of World Religions. 1997. *Encyclopedia.com*. (October 25, 2012). http://www.encyclopedia.com/doc/1O101-Sin.html

[21] Bowker, John. "Sin." The Concise Oxford Dictionary of World Religions. 1997. *Encyclopedia.com*. (October 25, 2012). http://www.encyclopedia.com/doc/1O101-Sin.html

[22] Bowker, John. "Sin." The Concise Oxford Dictionary of World Religions. 1997. *Encyclopedia.com*. (October 25, 2012). http://www.encyclopedia.com/doc/1O101-Sin.html

[23] "The Qur'an includes a version of the biblical story of the fall of Adam (Qur'an 7), but it does not conclude from it the doctrine of original sin as some Christian theologians have. In the Quranic version of the story, Adam and Eve begged God's forgiveness (7:23) and he punished them with a mortal life on earth but added, "from it [earth] you will be taken out at last" (7:25). Since Allah forgave the sins of the first pair, Muslims believe, all are born in *Al-Fitra*, a natural state of submission to Allah. True repentance from sin returns a person to this original sinless state"; *Islamic Beliefs about Human Nature*; http://www.religionfacts.com/islam/beliefs/human.htm.

[24] This phrase was coined by William Congreve, in *The Mourning Bride*, 1697.

[25] Numbers 5:31, 9:13, 18:22, 30:15; Ezekiel 16:58, 23:35, 23:49, 44:10, 44:12.

[26] *Newton's Third Law of Motion*; http://www.physicsclassroom.com/.

[27] How to grow impressive corn crop; http://www.doityourself.com/.

[28] *Sheol*; Merriam-Webster Collegiate Dictionary

[29] Meditation #17 by John Donne From Devotions upon Emergent Occasions (1623), XVII.

[30] Daring Greatly: How the Courage to Be Vulnerable Transforms the Way We Live, Love, Parent, and Lead; Brené Brown, Ph.D, LMSW; Gotham; 2012.

[31] Comments off the website www.bemorewithless.com.

[32] http://exilelifestyle.com/minimalism-explained/.

[33] Meditation #17 By John Donne From Devotions upon Emergent Occasions (1623), XVII.

[34] "One of the earliest forms of this saying goes back to Aesop's fable, *Hercules and the Waggoner*, where the moral of the story is 'the gods help them that help themselves.' The modern variant, 'God helps those who help themselves,' was allegedly first coined by the English political theorist Algernon Sidney and later popularized by Benjamin Franklin, a Deist. In case you're wondering, a Deist is one who believes that while a Supreme Being did indeed create the universe, that Supreme Being does not involve itself in human affairs. Therefore, miracles and special revelation (such as healing, prophecy, the virgin birth & resurrection of Jesus, and the inspiration of the Scriptures) don't actually happen"; www.bloggingtheologically.com/2009/07/08/everyday-theology-god-helps-those-who-help-themselves.

[35] *Over 46 million Americans live below poverty level*; Marketplace Morning Report for Tuesday, September 13, 2011; http://www.marketplace.org/topics/business/over-46-million-americans-live-below-poverty-level.

[36] *Suicide Rates Rise Sharply in U.S.*; By TARA PARKER-POPE; Published: May 2, 2013; http://www.nytimes.com/2013/05/03/health/suicide-rate-rises-sharply-in-us.html?_r=0.

[37] Steven Colbert; host of Comedy Central's *The Colbert Report*, a satirical news show in which Colbert portrays a caricatured version of conservative political pundits.

[38] *Mere Christianity*; C.S. Lewis; McMillan Publishers; 1952.

CPSIA information can be obtained at www.ICGtesting.com
Printed in the USA
BVOW01s0859080414

349954BV00003B/3/P